Is there a
book
in **you?**

Alison Baverstock

Is there a
book
in you?

Alison Baverstock

A & C Black

First published 2006
Reprinted 2006, 2007

A & C Black Publishers Limited
38 Soho Square
London W1D 3HB
www.acblack.com

ISBN-10: 0–7136–7932–8
ISBN-13: 978–0–7136–7932–8

A CIP catalogue record for this book is available from
the British Library.

Cover illustration and design © Michelle Radford 2006

Typeset in 10/12pt Sabon

Printed and bound in Great Britain by
Bookmarque Ltd, Croydon, Surrey

Contents

Acknowledgements

There are many people to thank for their time and wisdom in helping me write this book. As a child, Katharine Whitehorn's columns in *The Observer* were read aloud to me, by my father, as an example of good writing. I was thus completely delighted that she agreed to write the foreword – and did so overnight. I would also like to thank Dr Christopher Hand of the Kingston Business School for help with (I think the correct academic term is 'validating') my questionnaire; Catherine Lockerbie, Director of the Edinburgh Book Festival, who hosted the initial talk in August 2005; Sandy Williams, Director of the Kingston Readers' Festival, who allowed me to test my ideas out again; and the Society of Authors for ongoing help. The chapter on creativity drew on a 'Future Forecast' workshop organised by AN, the artists' information company. The audience at the Edinburgh event were very important to the creation of this book, so many thanks to them all – in particular to those who asked questions. I have also found an ideal publisher in A&C Black and would like to thank the entire team, especially Jenny Ridout, Jonathan Glasspool, Katie Taylor, Hilary Lissenden, Rosanna Bortoli, Jo Herbert and Vicky Harrison. Thanks to Edna Scott for proof-reading. More specifically I would like to thank the following:

Nicholas Allan; Fiona Allison; Hedi Argent; Trisha Ashley; Liz Attenborough; Sunil Badami; Francis Bickmore; Carole Blake; Hazel Broadfoot; Rev Simon Brocklehurst; Anne Brooke; Mark Brunsdon; Emma Burstall; Brian Cathcart; Professor Peter Checkland; Jane Cholmeley; Genevieve Clarke; Julie Cohen; Andrew Collins; Sheila Cornelius; Andrew Crofts; Molly Cutpurse; Emma Darwin; Aileen Davies; Edward Denison; Catherine Dell; Christian Dingwall; Cathy Douglas; Margaret Drabble; Helen Dunmore; Professor Robert East; Elizabeth Edmondson; Katie Fforde; Kerry Fowler; Helen Fraser; Judy Garton-Sprenger; Pauline Goodwin; Jenny Haddon; Stephen

Hancocks; Jill Hansel; John Harding; Pauline Harding; Brian Harper-Lewis; Roya Henry; Gill Hines; Alison Hogg; Heather Holden-Browne; Vanessa Howe; Dr John Hudson; Margaret Humfrey; Nicholas Humfrey; Professor Peter Humfrey; Gloria Hunniford; Margaret James; PD James; Professor Lisa Jardine; Dr Meg Jensen; Catherine Jones; Su Jones; Julie Kelford; Bee Kenchington; Mark le Fanu; Margaret Leroy; Jonathan Lloyd; Professor Wendy Lomax; Bernard Lyall; Sharon Maas; Jane Mays; Livi Michael; Richard Montgomery; Nicola Morgan; Julie Moss; Karen Mountney; Nicola Morgan; Wendy Orr; Jack Paterson; Wendy Perriam; Professor Gwyneth Pitt; James and Kate Plastow; Kate Pool; Adam Powley; Philip Pullman; John Ravenscroft; Jenny Ridout; Professor Michele Roberts; David Roche; Jane Rogers; Anne Rooney; Dr Anne Rowe; Kate Rowland; Sylvia Rowland; Anne Sebba; Harriet Smart; Esther Solomon; Jackie Steinitz; Mick Stephens; Alex Stevens; Kris Stuchbury; Rebecca Swift; Aline Templeton; Becky Todd; Stephen Torsi; Ion Trewin; Judge Martin Tucker; Alison Watson; John Whitley; Nicola Whitwell; Jacqueline Wilson; Moira Wilson; Louise Wirz; John Yarnall.

Finally, thanks to my family for their ongoing support, including tolerance of the 6.00 a.m wake-up in Edinburgh that began this book.

Foreword

How does anyone write a book? There's a saying that everyone has a book in them, but, even if it's true, that doesn't mean they know how to get it out – and I can't say I do. I have never written a book before – mini-books of 15,000 words or cookery books that can be written like journalism don't really count; and now that I'm trying to write a proper book – my autobiography – I am realising just how difficult it all is.

You might think I would know all about it, having been married half my life to Gavin Lyall, who wrote successful thrillers. I am certainly learning something of what he had to put up with. I now realise, for example, what drove Gavin frantic: the phone call from someone who wants to gossip just as you're getting the wording right; the domestic interruption; or the fact that everyone thinks that if what you are supposed to be getting on with is a book, it can always wait for a week or two, can't it? And then the weeks have gone by and nothing's been written and you get hysterical.

But no two writers, as far as I can tell, do it in the same way: there's absolutely no hard and fast pattern. One may write for a steady three hours each morning; another, in fits and starts. Simenon wrote each of the Maigret books in 16 days while his household padded fearfully around, hardly daring to breathe. Dumas, having finished a book at about 11 in the morning, apparently noted there was still some time before lunch and started another; while the author of *The Catcher in the Rye* took many years to begin – or at any rate to finish – another one. Truman Capote said the great thing was always to stop just before a bit you were going to enjoy writing – if you wait until you know the next bit's going to be distinctly tricky, you'll do anything you can think of to put off writing it at all. And doing things to put off writing is one thing all the authors I know do tend to be good at. Donald Carroll uses the term 'Work Avoidance Schemes' – the unaccountable urge to sort papers, check an unimportant fact, ring a long-forgotten cousin, make yet another cup of coffee.

But whether you do it regularly or haphazardly, fast or slowly, easily or with the most excruciating labour pains, the one thing that writers must have is the ability to get going on their own. Nobody is standing there telling you what to do; you are like a learner motor-cyclist, having to go solo from the start, with no white-knuckled instructor sitting at your side. There is no immediate deadline, no knocking-off time, and no manual.

Which is why, let's hope, this book may help writers to feel a bit less alone, a bit more encouraged. They may each have to paddle in their own way, but perhaps not so much in their own lonely canoe. It helps to realise that there are lots of other people – and sensible, talented people at that – who are all in the same boat.

Katharine Whitehorn
February 2006

Introduction

What this book is, and what it is not

"Reading books about writing is, in my experience, like reading books about sex: I'd rather be doing it."

Holly Brubach[1]

This book will not tell you how to write a novel – there are plenty of other titles available to tell you how to do that. Nor will it tell you how to improve your writing style, come up with a plot, or develop character – again, other sources of information exist. Indeed, as I did the research for this book I was surprised by just how many excellent writing resources there are for budding writers; for an activity I had always assumed you just got on with and did on your own.

What this book *will* do is to help you (and perhaps those around you) decide whether or not you want to try to write a book and get it published.

It will ask you key questions about your motivation and your staying-power, and highlight the key attributes that all writers must either have themselves, or be able to access. It is the product of my own experience – as a publisher, writer and reader. I like to think of it as the would-be writer's equivalent of the driving test. It will establish whether you are road-safe; whether or not you decide to go anywhere with it, is up to you.

My working title, which quickly became the real title, is of course a cliché, but one that seems to resonate very widely. The book began as a seminar for the Edinburgh Book Festival. I began my working life as a publisher, but have since written extensively about marketing within the book trade. I have given talks on

---

1 Reviewing Lynn Freed's book *Reading, Writing and Leaving Home* (see bibliography). *New York Times*, 9th October 2005.

marketing yourself as an author, and on the book trade in general, at the Festival for several years now, as part of *The Writing Business* series of events. For the 2005 Festival I came up with the idea of trying to define what it is that turns would-be writers into published writers. I identified a list of ten things and the seminar, with the same title as this book, was advertised. It clearly hit a nerve. Staff selling tickets told me it was the first writing event to sell out; we quickly sold 200 seats and had a waiting list for returns. And it was particularly interesting that the audience did not just consist of would-be writers; there were several members of the wide fraternity who try to support the writing – partners, children, parents and friends.

I circulated a questionnaire listing the ten attributes to everyone present, talked it through and then asked them to score themselves. We discussed the results. And, significantly, not a single copy of this questionnaire got left behind – clearly this was private information that people wanted to keep. Early the next morning (to the immense annoyance of my two older children who were sharing a room with me) I woke up with a flash of inspiration and decided there was another book that had to be written. I leapt out of bed, opened just one curtain, and started making notes. You are holding the result.

Why is the desire to write so strong? Whenever I have told other people what I am working on, the response is similar: a misty smile and a pause for reflection. The desire to write a book is a widely held ambition, and one that many people nurse for years. Some plan to write in their retirement; others try to write all the time, jotting down ideas whilst cooking, or sketching out full plots on the beach. JK Rowling famously outlined the entire scope of the Harry Potter novels while on a train journey from Edinburgh Waverley to London King's Cross. Others find the motivation to write in what they read, as much-publicised titles leave them feeling that *they* could have done better themselves. The key emotion aroused by the trumpeting of yet another new, young and beautiful writing talent is often jealousy.

But whereas many feel they could do it, the path to publication has never been easy, and any published writer will tell you to think carefully before you start. Writing is lonely; it involves long hours, hard graft, lots of rejection and (for most) only a slim financial reward. Whether it is you who wants to write, or someone you live with, my hope is that this book will show you whether or not you should consider trying – a valuable investment *before* you give up the day job!

Why should you trust me?

Because I have been through the process myself. I began my working life as a publisher; I have had several books published (this is number 14), and am a voracious reader. And along these various paths I think I have isolated several basic truths about the process of getting published that I maintain any would-be writer (or those supporting them) needs to consider. I will explain these factors, tell you how to work around or through them, and offer guidance (or solace) if your conclusion is that perhaps all the effort is just not worth it – and you would be happier gardening! I think many of us spend our lives on hamster wheels, trying to keep going, and just to step off occasionally and think about what you like doing and why, is a very useful exercise. In the process you might decide that your desire to write a book is in fact a real need for a more creative outlook on life, or a need for personal change.

No scientific (or pseudo-scientific) theory can be published without extensive testing. I have consulted a wide variety of writers, from the extremely famous to the aspiring, and offer their comments on the process of writing and being published. My questionnaire has been reviewed by colleagues at Kingston University's Business School as a worthwhile market-research exercise, and road-tested by many writers. Many have commented that it has helped them clarify *why* they kept going – what specific resources they have (perhaps never identified until now) that have helped them to achieve. It seems to hold water.

As well as expanding on my various themes, I have tried to address what to do if, after reading this, you feel you do *not* have a book in you. I remember one lady in particular at the Edinburgh event who said she had an interesting life with many friends, but could not think what to write about. My first response was predictable: I advised her to try examining interesting situations from someone else's point of view, or to spot incidents that had dramatic potential, and I quoted a few examples of books that had such origins. But thinking further after the event, I thought that perhaps my advice should have been for her to put her considerable energies into encouraging other people, and becoming a catalyst for stimulating book-related discussions – perhaps hosting a Scottish and 21st-century version of the literary salon – rather than feeling she had somehow failed by not knowing what to write about.

This book is not designed as a personal misery bucket, detailing all the pitfalls ahead. Rather, it is meant to help outline what resources you will need if you do decide that you want to be published. I think some understanding of what to expect in life is very helpful – it allows us to make choices; to help motivate ourselves when things do not go as planned, because we understand the wider picture. I have been an Army wife for long enough to know that while changes of plan often arrive extremely suddenly, the ability then to start planning around them always makes me feel better. Apparently rats and humans have this in common: we get depressed when we cannot plan for ourselves.

I hope this book will help you decide whether or not you are going to go for it – or get a life!

1

Just how much do you want to see your book in print?

This sounds like an obvious question. If you did not really want to write a book, you would not have bought – or been bought – this title.

You are not alone. The desire to write a book is shared by a huge percentage of the population. It's often said that everyone has at least one book in them – although wags have countered that this is often where it should stay. We seem to have become a society of writers rather than readers:

"There is an impression abroad that everyone has it in him to write one book; but if by this is implied a good book, that impression is false."

Somerset Maugham (1874–1965)

Why do we want to write?

"Many suffer from the incurable disease of writing, and it becomes chronic in their sick minds."

Juvenal (65?–128?), Roman poet

Some write to make sense of the world; to understand what has happened to them – for whatever life throws at you, understanding and dealing with it tends to become easier if you try to write about it. Others write to push their ideas out into the world; writing is a wonderful way of realising what you think about things:

"The pen is the tongue of the mind."

Cervantes (1547–1616)

1

> "For me, one of the great joys of writing is articulating something I have felt but never expressed before. The phrase 'coming to terms with' means precisely that: finding words to express the experience."
> Julia Bell, *The Creative Writing Course-book* (see bibliography)

Others write to make links with other people, to reach out:

> "Writing fiction is such a peculiar activity and often it can feel a foolish waste of time. But then I speak with a reader and find myself discussing the people I created and the world in which they live, and I realise both are as real to the reader as they are to me. That's a wonderful, magical feeling and it reminds me of the main reason I play this game: the fundamental desire to connect."
> John Ravenscroft

> "As soon as I started writing, I wanted to be published. I never even thought about just writing for myself. Writing, for me, is a way to connect with an audience. Self-expression doesn't feel real to me unless it communicates with somebody else. I can't even keep a journal unless it's on the Internet, where anyone can read it!"
> Julie Cohen

Composer John Rutter has spoken about his work as a way of making new friends; translations of books offer us the chance to communicate with people we will probably never meet, and could not talk to if we did.

Some writers use their books to put their particular point of view, without being cut short:

> "Writing is a way of talking without being interrupted."
> Jules Renard (1864–1910), French writer

Others wish either to rewrite history, or to get their own back:

> "Writers often use their books to pay off scores and dish the dirt. I know I do. It's the perfect opportunity: all the arguments, all the affronts done to you, outlined and articulated, and not a dissenting voice allowed."
> David Armstrong (see bibliography)

"I like to write when I feel spiteful: it's like having a good sneeze."
DH Lawrence (1885–1930), in a letter to Lady Cynthia Asquith

Writing also offers the tempting promise of a lasting reputation; a permanent contribution to life, which will outlast you. George Orwell gave as reasons for writing:

"… the desire to seem clever, to be talked about, to be remembered after death, to get your own back on grown-ups who subdued you in childhood."

And Professor Gwyneth Pitt:

"Two reactions to my first book were terrific. One was reading exam papers from the West Indies and finding my book referred to as authority. The second was going on a quality assurance visit to another university and meeting students – one of whom asked me out of the blue if I was the author of my book and said it had been the best thing he'd read as an undergraduate."

For some, writing a book can be a very pragmatic career choice, prolonging their 'shelf life'. The autobiographies of media stars, in whom there can be massive, but temporary, interest, can often be seen in this context. A book is longer-lasting and more permanently validating.

Books can also play an important part in representing ideas:

"The most important thing for me is that I've used my talents as a writer to enable the Ogoni people to confront their tormentors. I was not able to do it as a politican or a businessman. My writing did it. And it sure makes me feel good! I am mentally prepared for the worst, but hopeful for the best. I think I have the moral victory."
Ken Saro-Wiwa (1941–95), Nigerian writer and human rights activist[1]

Having a book published can also make us feel part of a community we either took for granted, or only felt partly attached to

1 See the work of English PEN, listed in the appendix to this book

before. It can be really surprising – and very motivating – to find out how many other people feel the same way you do. Liverpool author Helen Forrester has talked of her delight at being taken to the heart of the community after her books were widely read in the area where she grew up. Catherine Jones has offered Army wives a sense of the specialness of their lives through her books on Service life:

> "I got into writing by accident. I was persuaded by a friend to collaborate in a short humorous guide on how to be an Army wife, and the book *Gumboots and Pearls* did astoundingly well. We were amazed that all these women felt validated by the things we described. I carried on writing novels about Army wives."

And in addition to all these good reasons for writing, it can be so personally fulfilling:

> "I am convinced more and more day by day, that fine writing is next to fine doing, the top thing in the world."
>
> John Keats (1795–1821)

> "Writing is fantastically fulfilling. When it is going well, it's electrifying; as good as it gets. I write non-fiction, mostly science history. I am trying to explain complicated science to the person who perhaps does not want to know more than they need to in order to get the story. I have this image of what I write as a slide; that takes them to an understanding but without effort. And when I have done that, been able to come up with an analogy that works and makes a hard concept easy to understand, I feel a tremendous sense of achievement."
>
> Brian Cathcart

But given that so many people want to write, where, I have wondered, is the dividing line between those who dream of being published, and those who get into print? Of course there are many factors, and the incidence of luck is vital, but from talking to writers published and unpublished, it seems to originate partly in a sense of destiny, and partly in the determination to do something about it.

A sense of destiny

"I wasn't born until I started to write."

David Hare (b1947), playwright;
interview in *The Sunday Times* 11th February 1990

Successful writers have talked about their long-term and immense desire to get into print; to see their name on the front of a book. Some set themselves deadlines – I have heard Kazuo Ishiguro say that he saw his 30th birthday as the deadline by when he wanted to be published:

"When I was 25, I told myself that if I didn't get published by 30 and hadn't sold at least 250,000 copies, I'd give up. Of course, now I'm 31 and though published in newspapers and journals, am still working on that book ..."

Sunil Badami

Others set no deadline, but always wanted to be published:

"I have wanted to write books since I was at primary school. I liked the idea of part of my mind being embalmed between two covers."

Nicholas Allan

"I wanted to be a writer even when I was a young child. I used to make little books with stories and pictures in, and even sent one to a publisher when I was about ten. The publisher I chose had already gone bust, but I don't think that really affected my chances! I didn't set a deadline. I published my first book (which was an academic text) in my early 20s and have moved into writing much more interesting books since."

Anne Rooney

"I knew I was a writer from before I went to school. People always wanted to know what happened when I told a story. But I never really thought about being published until I had a book I was burning for people to read."

Jenny Haddon

"I always wanted to be a writer (well, a journalist, at any rate!), and can remember the toy typewriter my parents bought me for my tenth birthday. I invented a weekly newspaper, although cannot imagine what I found of interest in our boring suburban life to report on."

Anne Sebba

"From being a little girl I knew I wanted to be a writer and painter, though with hindsight focusing on being a rich writer and painter might have been a better idea. I don't know though – maybe being a rich writer and painter is a contradiction in terms? But anyway, here I am many years down the line, still writing and painting. My local newspaper started publishing my ghastly poems when I was about 11, and my very encouraging English teacher at school entered me in some kind of national children's writing playwriting competition, in which I was a runner-up. She also wangled me into six sessions of the typewriting course, so I can touch type, for which I will be eternally grateful to her."

Trisha Ashley

"I've wanted to write novels for as long as I can remember. As a little girl, I was always writing stories and once started a book – I must have been about 10 or 11 – but never finished it. I was totally immersed in it for a while though and I can remember the opening paragraph to this day!

I became a journalist and put all thoughts of novel writing to the back of my mind for years while I was busy working and having babies. Then one night I wrote the rough outline of a novel on the back of an envelope, which sat beside my bed for about a year. I thought I wouldn't get round to doing anything about it until my last child was at school. Then a kind friend, over lunch, basically encouraged me to get cracking, so I did. That was in June or July. The words just flowed, and by October I had a first draft. I set myself a deadline of finishing it by December – and I'm determined to meet it. Without a deadline, I could dither about for years more, which would make me very cross with myself."

Emma Burstall

As a child I myself was fascinated by book production, and at the age of nine I produced a series of titles with matching covers. I can still remember what they looked like – they had green paper covers, lined paper inside and three staples along the top. I confess too, that for some of the titles in this series, I even wrote the title and contents page and left the space for the text to be filled in later! So whilst the binding of the collected works of Alison Scott was more impressive than either the research or depth of observation, the desire to see my name on a book continued, and I longed for a Petite Typewriter and the standardisation it would bring to my writing (I never could decide on which handwriting style to adopt).

The determination to do it

"Open your eyes and look within.
Are you satisfied with the life you're living?"
Bob Marley (1945–81), Jamaican musician, singer and songwriter

Many may long to do it, but nothing will happen unless the writer really decides to engage with the process that Margaret Atwood has described as being like 'wrestling a greased pig in the dark'.

"I started writing because it was wet. Christmas had just finished in a depressing riot of meaningless indulgence, another year loomed, I'd just had an almighty row with my daughter and been admonished by my wife. The rain trickled depressingly down the window and I remember staring at it and thinking there must be more to life than this. So I started writing. After all, I'd been putting it off for 30 years.

It wasn't a structured start. I didn't have a plot or characters or anything much in mind other than some rambling thoughts and some hopelessly derivative stories I had told the children when they were young enough to snuggle into our bed on a Sunday morning. I could argue that I started writing in order to reach out to a daughter I felt I was losing touch with. But it would be a lie. I did it for me, because I was frustrated and bored, though making her into my heroine and getting her help with the story and plot development was a bridge of sorts when there was little else engaging us. So I just wrote in a sort of free-form way and waited to see what would emerge. And for once, I promised myself, I would see the process through and find out if I really could write.

And I did. I set myself weekly targets for words produced. I stuck to them. I indulged myself with endless rewrites when I got stuck. Going back always seemed easier, somehow, than going forward. I sent a couple of chapters to an agent and they were greeted with enthusiasm and encouragement. And about half way through the novel I felt it gather pace and momentum and then I was hooked. Finishing was easy after that."

John Whitley

"The crunch came in December 1988, when this tremendous yearning to do all the things I wanted just burst. I was frankly fed up with the financial world and responsibility. I had another world to conquer – the world of literature. When I left, I sold it all, good and bad. It wasn't a tough decision … You don't get anything without sacrifice in this world … [I was only able to be free again] after I was free of all the chains of ambition and responsibility I had put on myself. Exploration and writing released me from those bonds and gave me a second chance of living."

Lottie Moggach interviewing Christopher Ondaatje, businessman-turned-
writer in the *Weekend Financial Times* 22/23 October 2005

"The most important thing about actually getting to the end of my first book was proving to myself that I had the patience and stamina to do it. And to realise with some joy that I was doing something at 40 which I would never have been able to do at 30. There are precious few things one can say that about."

Bernard Lyall

"Aged 18, I found a holiday job working in the Arabic Department of the World Service doing nothing grander than filing tapes. But it was enough to say 'I've worked at the BBC' and, on the strength of that, plus my degree in History, I was accepted by REUTERS on a graduate trainee scheme – the first woman they had taken on this –

and began training as a journalist. While there I was sent to a publishing party and met a commissioning editor for Weidenfeld and Nicolson who uttered the magic words: 'Surely you've got a book in you, haven't you, all journalists do … Here's my card, come and see me on Monday …' Eight months pregnant, about to go on maternity leave, I knew this chance would not come twice – indeed, would not come about at all in the same way today.

So, with 48 hours to invent a best-selling idea, all I wanted to write was a biography of the French socialist Prime Minister, Leon Blum – of whom no one in England had heard and which would involve years of research in French archives. But Blum was my hero. So I prepared my case and went to meet my new best friend.

Weidenfeld and Nicholson in those days was housed in a rabbit warren of an office in Clapham. I puffed and panted up the eight floors and blurted out my idea with Enormous Confidence. That lovely man, John Curtis, was crestfallen. He obviously had such high hopes of me and knew this was a serious loser.

'Er. Any other ideas?'

On the spur of the moment I said: 'Well I have a small collection of antique needlework. Samplers, they're called.' I warmed to my theme. Nobody had written about American samplers, I told him. I had uttered the magic formula – America …

'Yes,' he said. 'Yes, I shall see if we can organise a co-edition.'

I wrote the book in a year. Once you have a first book the rest is, well never easy … John died of a sudden heart attack last year and I hope I said thank you adequately before he died.

Moral of the story? Go everywhere, talk to everyone. You never know."

Anne Sebba

That first book

Most writers can remember the arrival of the first copy of their first book in intimate detail. It's one of those flashbulb memories – like where you were when Elvis Presley or Princess Diana died. I am no exception. The package was thick and the postmark gave me a strong hint of what was likely to be inside. I stood in the hallway of our house, full of tension, as I tried to contain my desire to rip the packaging off – just in case I damaged the precious item underneath.

And then there was the incredible quietness of the moment itself. Finally, my name on the front of a properly bound book. It's been repeated since, and remains just as special each time; a moment of intense concentration when time really does stand still. One has usually seen the cover design already, but with the arrival of the book itself it is suddenly substantial: the physical embodiment of all those thoughts and all that effort; the smell of the paper, its surprising heaviness, your name on the front – and all these sensations underpinned by the thought that *I* really did do all that.

"Every single time I get the first copy of a new book, it feels just as wonderful as the first time. I just have to spend the day a) beaming b) carrying it in my handbag to show EVERYONE and c) stroking it."

Nicola Morgan

"I can remember every stage of my first book. Deciding I would write it and coming up with a structure that would work were satisfying, even more so when a publisher bought the idea. Then I remember finishing it and handing over a suitably heavy parcel to the publishers. I hand-delivered it to their magnificent offices in Albemarle Street – and then took myself off for a celebratory tea in Fortnum and Mason; the fact that it was my birthday made the whole thing even more special. It was well edited by Grant McIntyre and I was very pleased with the final product. I liked the cover and the substantial thump the first copy made on the kitchen table. It did not sell particularly well but that book has always had a very special place for me."

Brian Cathcart on *The Test of Greatness, Britain's struggle for the Atom Bomb*, John Murray, London 1994

"It's hard to describe my excitement at seeing my first book in print. I was excited enough when the galley proofs were delivered. My words! Typeset! What a thrill. I have now had four books published and every one of them feels special. Surely even Stephen King gets a kick out of seeing his books on the shelves. How could you not?

Even seeing them being sold second hand on Amazon for 29p excites me. Just to have books in circulation is exciting. I found it with a handwritten staff recommendation in a branch of Waterstone's only the other week, which excited me. It's a nice feeling to be *out there* in the world.

I love books. I buy way too many to actually comfortably read, but I just love owning them and having them and holding them. If you feel that way about books as a reader, it's inevitable you'll feel that way, times 100, about books with your name on the spine."

Andrew Collins

I dwell on this because most writers feel the same. Having a book published makes you feel significant. Correspondence columns and talk radio strive for instant notoriety – whether or not the opinions being expressed are reasonable or articulate. They are media that blare out rather than think carefully and represent. A book is different; other people are investing in your thought and writing, and that is validating. Ignore the snobbery of those who claim that their writing is not published because it is 'not commercial'; this is not a badge of honour. If what you write is commercial, it means that others want firstly to invest in it, and secondly to buy and then read it. For a writer these things are immensely validating.

"The first time I saw our book on the shelves was a bit of an ego boost. A customer picked up a copy and flicked through; rather pathetically I lurked in a corner of the shop to see what happened next but thankfully he bought a copy. I had to stop myself from cheering. To see a complete stranger prepared to pay good money to read your words is hugely satisfying – probably my proudest professional achievement."

Adam Powley

In part it is the compactness of it, seeing all your notes, crossings out and post-it notes condensed into one simple format, and there is the long-anticipated (but not always executed) joy of then throwing out all the previous versions, the piled-up printouts in your office: wonderfully cleansing! And all this is mixed with a feeling of admiration for the solidity of the achievement. The standard text inside pointing out that your 'right to be identified as the author of this work has been asserted' seems terribly important.

> "I love the fact that all those filing cabinets, all that mess, all those queries are now condensed into one beautifully produced book."
>
> Margaret Drabble on the *Oxford Companion to English Literature*, which she edited

> "Seeing the first copy of my book felt great – although the book looked quite small for all the work which had gone into it. I still love getting the first copies – but the biggest rush for me is when I send off the last bit of the copy to the publisher."
>
> Professor Gwyneth Pitt

> "Sometimes if I pick up one of my books and skim through it and see a bit I've forgotten about, I get a real tingle. 'Cor, did I really write that?' I think, and I feel quite proud of myself, although part of me wants to do a quick edit."
>
> Harriet Smart

> "Revisiting one's first book has a special poignancy, for it recalls that magical, wished-for, longed-for transformation of the aspirant writer into the 'real writer'. It glows in the memory with an aura of excited pride and innocent hope."
>
> David Lodge, from the foreword to the reissue of his first novel, *The Picturegoers*

But whilst the desire for publication must be present, if you want to be published you must be prepared to see it through; to give birth to the baby as well as to conceive the idea.

Many people have indeed described the production of a book as like having a baby – but it's more than that. My first four books were all written during pregnancy – in fact after four children my husband suggested that we find a new source of deadlines – but my books are my babies in a way that my children can never be.

From the moment a baby is born you realise that what has emerged is an individual. I can still remember the look our eldest child gave us at birth; he seemed to say: 'Now then, let's see what kind of choice I made.' Children are individuals, and whereas you can shape their development, and guide them, ultimately there is a spirit and a personality that will be its own person. A book, on the other hand, really is your own baby. It would not have come into existence without you and will carry the personality you gave it until you decide to update it or it goes out of print. On the other hand, whereas you can carry on trying to shape your child as it exhibits behaviour you are more or less comfortable with, the book you create will remain as you created it. Once it's 'out there', you can no longer shape or adapt it.

> "When I had my first book in my hands, I didn't believe that I had written it. Between manuscript and bound copy it had broken the umbilical cord. When I couldn't change it any more it stopped being mine."
>
> Jenny Haddon

Why does this pride in seeing your work in print matter?

It's important to isolate how you feel about seeing your name in print, because on the path to getting there, there will be many knock-backs. The world in general will be less impressed with your efforts than you are inclined to be, so if your determination to get there is strong, you stand a better chance of success.

One of the things that really interested me about finally having a book published was that, while I have never been so proud of anything in my life, the rest of the world was much less affected. Show a copy of your newly printed book to someone else, and nine out of ten people – even those whom you love dearly – will reply with one of the following (or a variation):

> "I've always felt there was a book in me, too."
> "That's something I have always meant to do."
> "I know someone else who has just written a book."
> "Lucky you, to have the time!"

Fifteen years after my first book came out, and 13 books later, I co-wrote a book.[2] My co-author had not written before, and whereas I warned her what to expect in most areas, I forgot about people's tendency not to admire the product. And the same thing happened to her: most of those she showed the book to responded with a comment that they, too, would one day do what she had done.

> "I did a reading recently in a school and looked after two classes for 90 minutes. The children loved it, responded well and were completely engaged. Their class teachers meanwhile sat at the back and chatted. They took no part in what I was doing. And when I came to leave, no one thanked me for my time, or commented that children had enjoyed it.
>
> As a former teacher, I am left with the distinct impression that my former colleagues are either jealous or think I have got too far above myself. I think it's a pity, writers should be encouraged, not put down."
>
> Children's author

Even those who have a vested interest in the product can seem quite cool in response to the announcement of its final existence. Publishers often respond to you finally finishing by being surprised that you have met your deadline – a bit like a midwife who has seen thousands of babies born, and who may become detached from the sense of achievement felt by the excited new parents. To continue with the parenting theme:

> "Books are babies that you live with for a very long time; they are so much a part of you for so long. And then all of a sudden you have to give them up, with no real sense that those you are giving them to value them at all. It can be incredibly frustrating to see the output of so much time and effort being delivered to people who seem to care so little – it's like an adoption with no contact agreement."
>
> Non-fiction author

> "Finishing a book is just like you took a child out in the back yard and shot it."
>
> Truman Capote

2 *Whatever! A Down-to-earth Guide to Parenting Teenagers* (Piatkus, 2005).

I mention this not to carp, but to warn potential authors. Your desire to get published must be yours alone; you cannot be pushed into it. Later chapters of this book will look at other ways of getting your name known, and selling books on the back of it. Here, I am assuming you are planning to write the book yourself. And there is no better fuel than your own motivation.

Do you have sufficient motivation to write a book?

I have described the special moment when you open up a package containing the first copy of your own book. While this is the goal that keeps many writers motivated, the day-to-day reality of a writer's life is much more prosaic.

> "There are always lots of reasons for not writing a book, whereas there are very few for embarking on an undertaking that's going to get difficult, will make you miserable, tired, anti-social and generally unhappy. And that's only the writing."
>
> David Armstrong (see bibliography)

In practice, getting published demands more than just a talent for writing. It requires you to be single-minded in pursuing your goal of publication, rather than half-heartedly thinking that 'some day I may get around to it'.

Those who have been on Creative Writing courses often acknowledge that it is not always the best writers who get the publishing contracts; often, it is those who are most determined.

Your 'stickability' quota

What is 'stickability'?

> "Endings are elusive, middles are nowhere to be found, but worst of all is to begin, to begin, to begin."
>
> Donald Barthelme (1831–89), US novelist and short story writer

15

The essential quality of stickability was first mentioned to me by my eight-year-old son's violin teacher. She said his approach to the instrument lacked it – and she was quite right. He would rather be outside playing football and getting him to practise was difficult. He gave up.

For a writer, stickability is essential. There are examples of works of literature that seem to stop and start at odd places: the opium-induced trance that famously produced Coleridge's *Kubla Khan* was famously interrupted by the 'person from Porlock', and Sylvia Plath's *The Bell Jar* always seems to stop very abruptly. However, most writers need to stick at their work until it is finished.

Authors not only need to make their output a whole, they then need to stick close by it (or to monitor the 'stickiness' of those representing their interests) in order to see it published. We will cover what you need to know about the publishing process later in the book, but for now it is worth pointing out that to be published, you must have a reputation as someone who is competent and reliable, delivering a quality manuscript on time. You also need to demonstrate an ability to produce the goods repeatedly – and many writers find this a great pressure. Being as good as your last book is hard, and the source of inspiration is not infinitely renewable.

> "Writing a whole book seemed an impossible undertaking and still does, if I let myself think about it while I'm in the middle. In fact that can frighten me so badly I stop writing."
>
> Jenny Haddon

A quick quiz on your 'stickability quota'

- Do you tend to give up easily?
- Do you tend to start on projects and then leave them half-way through?
- When did you last give up on a book?
- Would your family and friends describe you as determined?
- Do you make lists of things to do?

- How many do you manage to tick off each day, and how does being able to tick things off affect your mood?

- How carefully do you consider what goes on the list – does it consist of your priorities or those of others?

- Do you make plans for your career/personal ambitions/living circumstances? If so, how many do you see through?

Think back to your earliest experiences, and you may find some indicators. I had one particularly seminal experience at school, with a languages teacher whose tactic – which was not very consistent with today's teaching methodology – was to pounce on weak spots and isolate poor performance. If a wrong answer was provided, she would pursue the culprit until they cried, and then ignore them for the rest of the lesson; you did not forget again. From the start I was determined not to cry, and looking back I wonder if this signified an early streak of bloody-mindedness (or stickability).

> "A friend of mine at journalism school wanted to write for the *Guardian*. We all did – but not as much as her. Whereas I sent off a couple of pieces, then tried elsewhere, she stuck at it, and had sent them over 40 ideas by the time they took on her first. Moral: sticking at it if it matters enough to you does matter."
>
> Emma Burstall

In addition to sticking to things, we also need to be careful that we are sticking to the *right* things. A sense of business can fill our lives; meanwhile the great projects we meant to achieve never get any nearer. I suspect that writers who will end up being published can prioritise, put aside the trivia and get on with the writing, because nothing matters more to them.

> "I would advise would-be writers not to open their post or look at their emails until after their writing stint. It's all too easy to get diverted, distracted or thrown by a worrying letter or email. Also keep the phone on 'answer'. Leave the chores till later. Put your first and best energies into the writing itself."
>
> Wendy Perriam

17

"Would you rather be writing than doing anything else? This seems to me of fundamental importance."

Catherine Jones

Why a book?

Writing a book is seldom (or almost never; JK Rowling was *very* unusual) a speedy path to riches. More usually the life of the author is lonely, badly paid, lacking in solidarity and beset by disappointment. So before you plan your book, consider whether there are other ways in which your desire to create something permanent could be explored and brought to fruition. For example, could you:

- Create a garden?
- Decorate your house?
- Encourage other writers?
- Share your opinions, either through local discussion groups or through a local radio station?
- Take up a creative hobby such as pottery or painting?
- Do an Open University degree?
- Write letters to the local or national press and get satisfaction from this?
- Emphasise relationships and see more of your friends?
- Get fitter (Richard Adams has written about seeing exercise – in his case a long swim – as a 'physical creation'[3])?

Television and former *Blue Peter* presenter Caron Keating had a lifelong desire to explore fully the creative energy within her by producing something: perhaps through writing a book or concentrating on one of the art forms she experimented with, or through doing more media work. When critically ill with cancer she returned to the desire to write a book; but significantly the desire to produce something lasting was as important as the subject matter or format she would choose. As her diary reveals:

3 *The Girl in the Swing*, Penguin.

"Anxiety went and I felt much stronger. So much so, I decided I would like to work again: TV/radio/writing/painting. In truth what is my wish list – to write a book but then on what? Should it be about life in Byron [Australia], healing, what? Possible interview people for radio about spirituality, searching etc – suitable for Radio Four? Time for structure and getting on with life."[4]

You could always decide to preserve your memories in a different format, and forget about a commissioned book:

"I often advise people who ask me about publishing a memoir that, if they do not succeed in getting a publisher to produce their recollections, they should capture the memories in another way. For example, a tape recording of your life story will ensure your family know your story and also preserve your voice at the same time – something a book cannot do."

PD James

"When my readers say they want to write, and quite plainly from their letters are lousy at it, I try to stress that the mere act of writing is useful; in itself, even if you're only writing to get it off your chest or leave the family history for your grandchildren. This is partly to stop their being too disappointed if they aren't going to be published, but also I do believe it – just as all these retired people turning out bad watercolours all over Britain *are* doing the right thing – for them."

Katharine Whitehorn, journalist and agony aunt for *Saga Magazine*

"... *and home there's no returning* was initially written for the grandchildren and for pleasure. The book is a memorial to my brother, who was an officer on the battle cruiser *Hood*. He joined her at the beginning of her wartime career and went down with her in May 1941. During his service he sent 66 letters home; I have extracted bits I thought of general interest and have written an accompanying narrative. The book is unique because, as far as is known, no other letters have survived, certainly none have been published. I happened to show it to an historian attached to the HMS *Hood* Association and

4 11th March 2004 (just a month before she died), from *Next to You: Caron's Courage Remembered by Her Mother*, Gloria Hunniford, Penguin 2005.

he said it deserved a wider public. Now that it has been published I am very proud that the Admiralty Library regard it as 'a valuable addition to the Second World War biographies section'."

Bee Kenchinton, *... and home there's no returning*,
Arcturus Press, Fleet Hargate, Lincs

"After 27 rejections, ten from publishers and a further 17 from agents, I have now crossed the Rubicon into self publishing. I have written the story of my family. In particular of my mother's travels to India and round the world with her irascible father (who went to India as a piano tuner aged 19) of which Mark Tully wrote 'you have a wonderful story to tell'. The material I had at my disposal (which began with a batch of letters discovered after my mother's death) and the additional research I did compares well with the family memoirs of Blake Morrison, Simon Garfield and John Mortimer. But I am a 75-year-old one-book man, and publishing my book commercially is seen as a useless investment by the large firms. At least through self-publishing my work will be formally preserved and my grandchildren will be able to see what an interesting family they come from."

Judge Martin Tucker, *The Chingri Khal Chronicles*

"Towards the end of my father's working life, he and my mother commissioned Graham Clarke to produce a cartoon-style picture of the house they have lived in for the past 20 years. This type of historical picture used to be a common way of recording family heritage in earlier times. The picture reflected their married life and the early married life of their children, with various grandchildren and dogs sprinkled around the garden, and scenes relevant to our lives around the edge. It is a compilation of their lives, and those of their families. They have the original image, and a limited edition of ten further copies were made, one for each of the children, and sufficient to pass on to grandchildren and great-grandchildren that may appear. They got enormous satisfaction from re-visiting the past and thinking about what should go into the picture, and it is such a special thing for us all to own."

James Plastow

"The world of writing is full of many valid and functional parts, and being published by a London publishing house may not be the best route to your ideal audience. If you really want people to read your work, give it to your friends, read it out loud in a pub, publish it in a small magazine. Dip your toes in the water tentatively, don't be dazzled by Lottery-like dreams of millions; the glittering prizes come to a very small percentage of writers. You think writers are glamorous? Go and see them read. They're usually on the edges of poverty, badly dressed, in need of a haircut, slightly red-eyed from too many late nights and too much coffee."

Julia Bell, *The Creative Writing Course-book* (see bibliography)

Questionnaire

Now turn to the questionnaire at the back of the book and think in detail about how much you want to write a book. As you think about this, bear in mind that the writer's life is lonely; that other people will put you down; that there is huge competition to get published; and that there is little solidarity among the writing community – a good idea can always be offered to someone else in the hope that they will do it cheaper. Then there are ideas that are just in the ether for all to access – part of the prevailing Zeitgeist – and someone else may quite reasonably arrive at the same idea as you. That will not reduce the feeling of intense jealousy you suffer if someone else comes up with your idea and gets to print first.

"Writing is not a profession but a vocation of unhappiness."

Georges Simenon (1903–89), creator of the detective, Maigret

Think about how long you have wanted to write a book for, and what part it plays in your personal agenda. How much would having a book published matter in the long term? Is it something you would put on your gravestone, or do you feel as the first woman who won *Mastermind* commented, when asked if it would change her life: "Of course not – it's not that important."

When you have thought long and hard, give yourself a mark out of ten for your commitment to seeing your book in print.

2

How much do other people like reading what you write?

So can you write? This sounds blindingly obvious, and is irrelevant if you are writing purely for your own pleasure. Provided you can read your own handwriting, and the writing materials you have chosen are as durable as you need them to be, you may be detained here no further.

But for what I suspect is the vast majority of my readers – those who are reading this book in order to present writing for other people to read – the key question is not, 'Can you write?' but, 'Do other people want to read what you have written?'

The answer is long and complicated. No single style of writing will ensure that what you write is well received. People who read *The Daily Telegraph* or the *Financial Times* every morning may like to relax with *Hello* or *FHM* at weekends. Writing is heavily subject to the influence of fashion, and just as models can find themselves out of work because they have 'last year's face', so what may have been publishable last year is now seen as old hat. There is no one style that will guarantee a readership. The writing equivalent of BBC English was standard for many years, but today publishers have become much more open to the possibility of printing books in colloquial English to appeal to specific market sectors, whether they are based on age, geography, culture, race or sex. Books can work on different levels, and be profitable on a smaller scale:

> "No one says a novel has to be one thing. It can be anything it wants to be, a vaudeville show, the six o'clock news, the mumblings of wild men saddled by demons."
>
> Ishmael Reed (b1938), US writer

Having stated how wide the goalposts are, it is helpful to provide guidance on what those who are making decisions about whether or not to publish you will be thinking. How do they decide whether other people will want to read what you write?

How do they decide?

There follow the views of agents, publishers, retailers, librarians, reviewers, book group members and Creative Writing tutors.

The agent

"When I receive sample material from a potential new author, I look for evidence that I am dealing with a writer – someone who believes in their material and writes with a sense of conviction. An obvious point, you might think – but too many writers write with tongue in cheek, or think that a gimmicky plot is all that matters. Also I want to represent writers who are planning a career in writing. I never take on one-off clients.

I look for the writer's ability to involve me quickly in the characters, the atmosphere and the storyline. Good storytelling encourages the reader to relax into it.

In the first few pages, I look for the ability to handle material in a way that suggests the writer could carry off a whole novel and is in charge of the characters and the backcloth. I want to find evidence that the writer has confidence and can handle emotion and pace. I need to see that the characters develop realistically within the course of the story. Characters who suddenly change direction and attitude are seldom believable. The storyline has to be set up in a way that makes their actions wholly credible."

Carole Blake, *From Pitch to Publication* (see bibliography)

"The best non-fiction engages me immediately, even if its subject is unfamiliar. It is clear, vivid, as fluent as the best fiction and its style and sentences are appropriate to the subject; so a history book will avoid jarring modern language but a contemporary autobiography will sing with the person and place of its writer."

Heather Holden-Brown

The Publisher

The general publisher

"Most editors have catholic tastes, and I am no exception. One of the joys of commissioning is never knowing where the next great book is coming from. I remember receiving the diaries of Field Marshall Lord Alanbrooke (Chief of the General Staff during much of WWII). It was a large script, but within a few pages I could feel the hairs tingling on my neck. Not only did Alanbrooke write well, but here was Britain's top soldier demonstrating that he could and did stand up to Winston Churchill in the conduct of the war. *War Diaries 1939–45*, as we titled the volume, was also history at first hand – what better! The editors, Alex Danchev and Dan Todman, had done a superb job and I had absolutely no doubt that we had a bestseller on our hands (which proved to be the case!).

Something very different: a few years ago Edna O'Brien told me over supper that she was absorbed by the shocking and true story of a murder of a young woman and her son on the west coast of Ireland. The murderer, a young man, buried the corpses in a forest clearing. He was soon arrested, tried and jailed. Edna wrote the story as fiction to get inside the mind of the murderer. When she gave me the typescript I was gripped from page one to the end, even though I knew the outcome. Here was a fine writer inspired by her material and at the top of her game. In Ireland, *In the Forest* split the nation – those who objected to what they saw as Edna's intrusion were in the end out-flanked by those, like me, who felt we needed to understand the whys and wherefores of such a ghastly deed – and a novelist is often far superior to any psychiatrist at so doing."

Ion Trewin, Editor-in-chief, Weidenfeld and Nicholson

The specialist publisher

"Our books fall roughly into two groups: trade (low-priced sold predominantly through retail) and professional/academic (sold both direct and through retail). In both instances the most important success factor is that the author knows his/her market. Literary merit is not that important these days, I'm afraid. In the case of trade books, unless the author has a high profile, is media savvy, can raise endorsements from 'names', has great connections, is on the speaking circuit, etc., it won't run. In the case of professional/academic titles, they have to be carefully aligned to a particular course/syllabus, or produced in association with a professional body or corporate organisation which recommends them or places a bulk purchase. In other words, you must be sure the market exists or your risk is underwritten first. All authors must have their own websites.

We no longer take risks, largely because there is little support from the trade. So my advice to any prospective author who wants to make an immediate impression on a non-fiction publisher such as Kogan Page is to show them that you know: your market; your routes to market; your competition; your media; how to sell yourself and your product; your product offering – its features and benefits. And UK authors need to take a lead from US authors who excel in proposal submissions; their market knowledge is superb, as are their presentation skills. I suppose it's a culture thing."

· Pauline Goodwin, Senior Publishing Director, Kogan Page Ltd.

The retailer

"The job of the retailer is made complicated by the simple 'quart into a pint pot' inequality that results from well in excess of 100,000 new books coming out every year, when the average shop can only stock around 30–40% of this number. This limited capacity is further reduced by the need to maintain availability of proven backlist titles which sell perennially.

As a result the buyer inevitably has to filter new material with a finer mesh than they, or the publisher, would like. This in turn means that the publishers will push harder for the titles that have cost them the most, and this does not always line up with the best books that they have the responsibility to present.

The only way to overcome this and successfully pan for gold is to read as much of the new material as is feasible, bearing in mind that it is impossible to read everything that comes in. The biggest shock to the system is being forced into sampling books and making a relatively quick decision, say within the first 30 or 40 pages, as to the potential of the book. 'Do I want to finish this book and find out what happened?' Ditch or date – but would *Captain Correlli's Mandolin* have passed this ungainly test? The style and quality of writing is an important factor but 'is it commercial?' and 'will it sell?' are questions that also have to be answered, while also bearing in mind the breadth of tastes that are held by the cross-section of customers that visit book stores.

However it only takes one evangelist to get the ball rolling. So getting proofs early into the hands of tastemakers, at either head office or in stores, is therefore vital. Books like Carlos Ruiz Zafon's *Shadow of the Wind*, Alice Sebold's Lovely Bones, Mark Haddon's *Curious Incident of the Dog in the Night Time* and Yann Martell's Booker Prize winning *Life of Pi* are good examples of where book-sellers' enthusiasm and recommendations helped to raise the profile of the books. Once initial sales levels put the books in enough hands that critical mass is reached, then quality will win out, and the most powerful force of all – personal recommendation – will take over. Awards are the icing on the cake.

The successful retailer will ensure that their network to identify new winners is as extensive as possible and that lines of communication are quick and clear. In this way a local success can be extrapolated across the country in a remarkably short space of time."

David Roche, BA President

The independent retailer

"Choosing stock from the many thousands published every year is difficult for an independent bookshop. We are challenged for space, so there is little luxury for making wrong decisions. Every book that's held in stock has to justify its place. Our reputation for good service rests very largely on the success of the recommendations that we make to our customers, so we take a lot of trouble to get them right.

We all read widely, both adult and children's books. The titles that we choose for special promotions tend to be ones that one of our team has read, and felt passionately about. They could be something that we've read about in the newspapers or, more usually, the trade press – something that we've seen in the publishers' catalogues or advance proof copies supplied by the publisher or their rep. They will not necessarily be the books that publishers are focusing the biggest promotional spend on – we choose what we know is right for our market.

Once we've chosen a book it gets our whole-hearted support. It's advertised both inside and outside the shop as a Book of the Month and we recommend it to as many people as possible. We know that our support can make a difference to a title at a national level. Some time ago we received a proof copy of a first novel for teenagers called *A Gathering Light*, by Jennifer Donnelly, published by Bloomsbury. We were stunned by how good it was, and gave it our full backing. We sold around 100 copies in hardback, which we rated as highly successful.

Subsequently we discussed our promotion in a speech at the Booksellers' Association Annual Conference, which brought the novel to the attention of the Richard and Judy team. It was chosen as one of their featured titles, and went on to sell in huge quantities. The novel subsequently won the Carnegie Medal, one of the most prestigious children's book awards. We know that our support helped this book, and we were delighted when that was recognised by Bloomsbury. When Jennifer Donnelly came to England to collect the Carnegie, they brought her to our shop to sign copies – a great coup for a small independent.

A small review in *The Daily Telegraph* drew our attention to *The Sixth Lamentation* by first-time author William Brodrick. We thought it an excellent read and began promoting it heavily. Part of our support was to tell other people in the book trade: ours was one of a few voices which recommended the book to the Richard and Judy team, and the book featured in their summer reading strand. This is not meant to suggest that we have a hotline to Richard and Judy – we don't. I simply want to illustrate how important word of mouth is in building titles. Word of mouth from booksellers and customers can create the most powerful effect on a book's sales and can be more effective than the most expensive advertising campaign. The history of *Captain Corelli's Mandolin* and *The Kite Runner* demonstrates the point perfectly. The passionate support of booksellers, whether independent or not, can be enormously beneficial to sales."

Hazel Broadfoot, Co-owner of The Bookshop,
Dulwich Village, and Beckett's Bookshop

The specialist retailer

"How early do you get involved? Not particularly soon. For most retailers their first sight of a book comes with the rep selling it in to you, although if you are lucky you may be given a proof copy to read, so we do rely very much on what the publishers tell us. This may be different for the buyers at big chains, whom I know can have an influence on jacket design and do get consulted much earlier in the process.

When deciding to back a title, obviously you use your experience to match the title (format, price, author track record, popularity of subject, competition, etc.) to your clientele. I remember in the early days of Silver Moon a gentleman rep sitting down and asking me what sort of shop we were, so I carefully explained our remit and then he tried to sell me a whole list of football and other sport books. Perhaps he had not been listening.

The best bit – the bit where being a bookseller can be like Christmas; where the crusading passion and the feeling that even you, as a small business owner, can make a difference – comes when you find a book you love and feel strongly about; one you can really promote. In this era of '3 for 2', of money off and head-office promotions, I have always found that the genuine staff recommendation is a thousand times better. It comes with real feeling and is unsullied by money changing hands. There's nothing like the feeling when a customer comes to the till with a stack of books you have recommended and can talk about. It is like giving a gift, the gift of sharing something you have loved with another. No wonder we say that selling books is *not* like selling baked beans (although the pay is similar!).

As for examples of where we have successfully got behind books and sold them, my co-founder of Silver Moon, Sue Butterworth, sold 58 copies of a Bernice Rubens paperback book about the Holocaust, which she felt was important; normal sales would have been about two or three. We put all our efforts behind a Margaret Atwood title with window displays, and an event, and sold 360 hardbacks in one night. Later, when working for a chain, I once did a survey on the respective sales rates between staff recommendations and head-office-promoted titles, and found the former outsold the latter by a factor of at least 10:1 – and this was at full price."

Jane Cholmeley, co-founder of Silver Moon,
formerly of the Charing Cross Road, now part of Foyles

The librarian

"I am one of five librarians who select the stock for the seven libraries in the Borough. I buy adult fiction and non-fiction for one of the small community libraries. We have an understanding of who are our most regular users, but we also want to encourage a wider accessing of our service, and to tempt those who have not used the library before to come in too. New books are an essential part of what we offer.

It's difficult deciding which titles to stock. If my budget were unlimited I would buy a copy of everything, as every book has been produced for a reason, and so there will be potential readers for each title. But funds are limited and I have to select titles that will appeal to as many readers and their interests as possible.

Making choices is difficult because we no longer view an 'approvals collection' of new books, where we get to examine the books physically. Now most of our buying is done online – we look at a synopsis and the cover, but don't get the chance to read a few paragraphs, or to handle it, before deciding whether or not to stock it. I keep up to date with the professional literature, read reviews and the previews in *The Bookseller*, and of course read widely myself, but it can be difficult to get a sense of what a book is like from its cover and the basic information provided. My main responsibility is Reader Development; this involves trying to encourage readers out of their usual 'comfort zones' and to try and choose something different, so I have to anticipate what they may enjoy, as well as buy what I know they already do. Popular, well-known authors select themselves, but getting a sense of what a first novel is like, without the book in front of you, is much more difficult. Some library authorities have moved to central buying based on local stock profiles. This obviously saves time, and hence money, but vastly reduces the amount of skill involved in selecting for the local community – and our feeling that we are meeting our readers' needs.

Covers matter enormously. Obviously they are one of the things we do see for a new book (the image is shown on the screen we see), but because libraries are heavily into promoting as well as stocking books these days, many are displayed in the library face out, rather than spine on. Sometimes a book jacket does not do justice to a particular title, which won't encourage readers to pick it up and try it. While the quality of the writing matters more than the cover, often the jacket design would never have drawn the reader's attention to look at the book. Displays and reader review comments play an important part in encouraging readers to choose something new to read. I make the selections for the various book groups that run throughout the Borough and people often comment that they have enjoyed something that they would not have picked it up without our recommendation.

I try to match the format I choose for our local libraries to the local population. For one community I buy mostly paperbacks; for another, hardbacks, depending on what the regular users appreciate."

Fiona Allison

Children's librarian

"I am a children's librarian buying books for the 11–18 age group. Obviously this age span covers a huge range of interests and reading levels, although everything I buy gets stocked in the same section of the library.

I still choose the books by looking at an approvals collection – I like to see the physical products I am buying, rather than choosing online, although I am aware that I am part of a dying breed and more and more purchasing is done in this way. What I choose comes from a wide variety of sources. I don't have children myself but I try to read as many of the relevant titles as possible, and then of course I read reviews. What matters most, though, is what children tell me they are enjoying. I have a job-share and between my colleague and I we run nine book clubs in local schools. I love to hear what the kids are passionate about: if they like one author they will tend to read everything they have written. I also try to access the websites on which children review titles. I don't particularly rely on publisher reputation (although I do trust Bloomsbury) and will buy from any publisher if the book looks interesting and is right for the age group. I tend to steer clear of 'issues' type books which children can find patronising and artificial. I would rather a see a particular issue well handled through good fiction, with a strong story and well-developed characters; books that just concentrate on the issues alone can seem quite cold. If a particular title gets requested, provided it's not too expensive, we buy it.

The covers are not particularly important. I tend to go on author reputation, and, if I trust an author to write well for this age group, I will buy even if the cover is poor. I do have to buy a lot of books that appeal to this age group that are not necessarily brilliantly written – mostly television tie-ins – because that is what the kids want to read; in the process, however, we can turn them into regular readers if we encourage them to try other things afterwards.

As regards controversy over what we buy, people seem more willing to complain about all sorts of things these days, but I would rather they were reading than not. You have to be careful how you classify things in libraries, but the chances are that if children are coming in and wanting to read the more adult titles, their reading ages are higher – and perhaps their maturity greater – than might be apparent from their chronological age. While we have to take note of particular group and religious sensitivities, I do feel too that once kids are at secondary school, they are reading Shakespeare – which is full of sex and violence – so we should not be too squeamish. If we only offer them bland material, which offends no one, we risk putting them off reading altogether.

Reading is such a good starting point for discussion. I love being with the children and hearing their opinions – with which they are packed!"

Vanessa Howe

The reviewer

"It's not so much a stunning first paragraph that pulls me into a book, as pace, an engaging voice and seamless storytelling. If I can pick up a novel and be on the fourth or fifth page without noticing how I got there, that is the litmus test: I am engaged temporarily in another world. With some exceptions – robots, very rude sex, and rugby, say – anything goes in the way of subject matter for the books I review for *Good Housekeeping*.

Women have much less time to sit down with a good book now, and when they do they often want immediate connection – with the characters, the story, the backdrop. Commercially, everyday school-run mums and their chums, or three-friends-in-emotional-crisis scenarios do work and they do sell. But so do stories of women who can't love their children, dysfunctional families, angry, betrayed lost people who find their way – or maybe not. Snapshots of life, sagas, situations we can relate to and sometimes be glad we're not part of – whatever path your book takes, it has to charm the reader into wanting to know more.

If you want to make your mark, then dare to be bold, follow your original middle-of-the-night inspiration, and run it through with emotional strands you know others will love to read about. The subject can be as controversial or average as you like – what matters is that you have an original voice and feel passionate that someone else should hear it."

Kerry Fowler, Reviews Editor, *Good Housekeeping*

Reading groups

The rise on rise of the reading group in the UK is having a huge impact on what is bought, and increasingly on what is commissioned. Publishers are very conscious of what will sell to this market, and the need to communicate with it – hence the variety of newsletters and websites that have been set up with this aim in mind. The choice of what is read by each group is often a detailed process.

"Choosing the book for the month is not a job to be undertaken lightly. With ten people about to spend many hours reading the book, it represents a lot of wasted 'woman hours' if no-one appreciates it. My husband always suggests books that he thinks would be 'improving' for the group – typically something scientific or historical. However, I think that the optimum choice is a book that is both enjoyable to read and one which stimulates a good discussion, even controversy, at the book group evening. Our group has now read over 80 books so we speak from experience when we say that books that were pleasant but bland do not make for such a rewarding evening. Conversely it is not unusual, after an evening spent discussing a book, for members to say they want to reread it, even if they didn't enjoy it the first time through, as the discussion opened up new avenues for them.

The group rules are that we must choose a paperback we have not read before, and one which we would like to read ourselves – though I don't take the part about wanting to read it myself too literally. It is important that the whole group will get something from the choice, even if they fall short of actually liking the book.

Generally I take a multi-pronged approach to choosing. I often ask friends in other book groups what they have enjoyed recently. I also look on the Internet at a number of sites (we have links to them on our own website, www.kingstonbookgroup.com) to see what books are being recommended. I particularly enjoy a site by another group called the Book Bags! If I'm organised I may have kept some of the supplements that generally appear in newspapers just before the summer holidays and Christmas about recommended reading for the season. Once I have a shortlist of possibles I like to look through the reviews on Amazon – though obviously these have to be read with caution; the reviewer may well be the author's mother. Finally I never choose a book without looking at it in a bookshop and skim-reading the covers, the reviews and a few extracts. Typically I end up choosing the book that had been first choice on my shortlist. But if there is anything that rings warning bells – my personal pet hates, for example, tend to be books in the present tense, or books with unreadable typography (we read one in the group with no paragraphs which was right-justified throughout) – then I will turn to number two on the list. Contrary to the maxim that you can't judge a book by its cover, I do think that a good cover can enhance reading pleasure. I felt happy every time I picked up the bright sky-blue and yellow cover of *Driving Over Lemons*. Hopefully, with all this research, the choice will be a good one!"

Jackie Steinitz

"How do I go about choosing books for our reading group? There is one thing that does not influence my choice of books – a review. I am a voracious reader, but I am afraid to say that I never read book reviews in the papers. The following all do influence my choice:

- I am a great fan of libraries and probably visit one several times a week. The library near where I work (Shoe Lane) has some excellent displays: 'books to select if you are in a rush', 'classic books that you should have read', etc. I often look at these shelves for initial ideas, and always look in the 'returned' section in libraries – I find it interesting to see what other people have read.

- I take an interest in books that have featured in prizes. I like to read a selection of books that have been shortlisted for the Orange prize.

- In terms of deciding why to pick a book off the shelf, I am influenced by the book cover; I read the plot information and the information about the author to understand a bit of background, although I very rarely read the publisher's comments. A prime example of books that I have bought because of the cover are Maria Lewycka's *A Short History of Tractors in Ukrainian* and Andrey Karkov's *Death and the Penguin*. You can almost tell by the cover if a book is aiming for the book circle audience – I try to avoid these ones and deliberately never choose any book if I hear a friend at school say 'our book circle is reading it'.

- I like to choose books that balance the choices of others in the book circle. There is a tendency to choose modern literature; I try to think of a balance and often seem to choose older, more classic books – not because these are the only books I read.

- I select books that I would not necessarily choose to read in my 'spare time' – for example, I often choose books that I have wanted to read but couldn't get into, or which simply fell to the bottom of my reading list."

Becky Todd

Admissions tutors on Creative Writing courses

"It's hard to say precisely what you are looking for – really, something that grabs you. That probably includes original ideas, presented in an original way. We look at how the writing has been constructed, and in particular if the narrative form works, together with register, diction, pacing and the like. We look at whether presentation is professional and basic grammatical issues are addressed – or, if they diverge from the norm, that they are handled consistently. These are quantifiable skills which all writers will have to a greater or lesser degree, and which can be improved upon through courses such as ours. While it is impossible to define what comprises good writing – because this is a very subjective area and tastes differ – we are clear about what makes writing good enough to allow for admission to the MA."

Dr Meg Jensen, Head of Creative Writing, Kingston University

"What am I looking for? It's easier to say what I'm *not* looking for; no clichés, either of style or content; no tired and over-used topics, particularly stories with a depressed first-person narrator (often adolescent or a student) to whom not very much happens.

The two qualities I am looking for above all are an interest in language, and using it well; and evidence that narrative, in the form of suspense, conflict, *a story*, is present in some form. It is good to find both of these qualities in a piece of work, but certainly possible to work with a student whose work has one but not the other. Without either, I'm afraid the applicant does not get far."

Jane Rogers, Course Leader for 'Novel'
on the MA in Writing at Sheffield Hallam

How you decide whether creative writing is any good or not is an issue that those teaching the subject have to grapple with all the time. Of course, students have to be assessed as part of the formal processes of an academic institution, and the marks awarded must stand up to scrutiny and challenge (ever more important at a time when study can incur debt).

A group of writers involved in this process for the National Association of Writers in Education[1] have attempted to isolate the elements of good writing in any form or genre, and to describe a sliding scale of achievement in each element. The criteria apply equally to poetry, prose and drama, and are as follows:

1 Ann Atkinson, Liz Cashdan, Livi Michael and Ian Pople.

Language	Control of the language – especially adjectives, adverbs and cliché
Observation	The discerning of details which render situations vivid to the reader; the principle of 'showing, not telling'
Structure	The organisation of text with the needs of genre, reader, content and economy in mind
Voice	Control of narrative voice dialogue, register and tone; may well be 'achieved' as against 'innate' and, thus, is linked to observation
Commentary/analysis	The student's own exploration of their writing portfolio, which engages with the four other assessment criteria, through redrafting and editing

A final important point to make is that all the above are individuals, and one must not underestimate the impact of personality on choice. Choices of what to publish are often based on criteria other than the quality of the writing: work may be commissioned to meet a larger but as yet largely unserved market, even though another submission may be argued to be 'better written'.

"… what makes good or great writing is not the simple ability to follow habits and customs; it's the presence of a strong and original vision that employs writing as a medium of exploration."

Malcolm Bradbury, introduction to Dorthea Brande's
Becoming a Writer (see bibliography)

How other writers assess what they are reading

"The great Samuel Johnson seldom began a book at the beginning. He started in the middle and went back to the beginning if it was any good, that way you don't waste time. I never struggle with a book because if I'm bored, I stop. I'm quite often not in the mood for a book, so I abandon it."

AN Wilson, commenting on Victoria Beckham's tendency not to finish books in *The Daily Telegraph*, 1st September 2005

"As you get older you become more impatient with wasting any time, so I'm quite ruthless with novels. If a novel doesn't really grip me I have no compunction about throwing it aside."

Andrew Marr, journalist, ibid

"This is not a novel to be tossed aside lightly. It should be thrown with great force."

Dorothy Parker (1893–1967), US writer and wit

Summary

By way of summary, someone may be seen as capable of writing for potential publication if their work:

- is interesting and involving
- feels innovative
- sparks an empathy in the reader
- arouses involvement, not critique. If you stop looking at it as writing to be analysed, and get sucked into the content, this is perhaps the best proof of an ability to write for publication.

How to prove you can write – by doing it

Here's a very basic piece of advice. You are more likely to end up with a book with your name on the cover if you start by writing other things first.

We know already that there are literally millions of people who feel there is a book in them. The best way of encouraging yours out of you and onto the bookseller's shelves is to build both your confidence and your habit as a writer – and that is best done by writing for publication.

Getting into print, in whatever format, offers the following:

Proof that you can write

Getting your name in print, whether you write articles in the parish magazine or the local paper, or for a national broadsheet, is proof that other people want to read what you have to say. The simplest organisational newsletter will probably have some editorial standards, and the fact that they are willing to offer space to your connected words places an objective and external value on your work.

If what you write generates correspondence – letters to the editor, feedback pieces from other writers – all the better. Store away the proof that not only can you write, but others read and respond to what you say.

Proof that you can complete something

Many want to write; few have the determination to do so. A selection of cuttings attached to a submission shows a gutsy determination to get published.

The 'buzz' of seeing your name in print

Let's be frank: it's wonderful to see your work in print. Nothing is better for boosting your sense of self as a writer.

My first articles were written for a garrison newsletter in Osnabrück, then in West Germany, where we were stationed. Having met the editor at a coffee morning, and heard she was looking for contributions, I decided to have a go. I suggested a series of features on local places of interest, and she agreed. Each month I wrote about somewhere to go at weekends and illustrated my articles with happy snaps taken at the same time. I placed a particular importance on pleasant places to go for tea. The magazine was professionally typeset and printed, with a circulation of about 2,000. But each time the magazine popped through my door I barely noticed the rest of the content, so focused was I on how my piece read, and how good it looked in print. My brother (now a sports journalist) made his writing début in the *Harts Hotspur*, magazine of the Potten End Football team, which was written by him and typed up by the mother of another player. Circulation approximately 30 – but now considered a collector's item by his friends!

There is a huge pleasure that comes from other people reading what you have written and recognising you as someone who can write. Don't underestimate how satisfying this can be.

Options for publication – other than a book

Just because your day begins with a glance through a national newspaper, don't assume that this is the only place worth being published. You could also consider the following:

Family newsletters
The round-robin Christmas letter is a source of much festive merriment, but a well-written missive can be an immense source of pleasure – and a very good way of impressing a group of people (who are likely to be sympathetic to you), with important evidence that you really can write. I confess that I do write one, and people have been kind enough to say they look forward to receiving it. In my own experience, the key thing is not to take yourself too seriously, and to include more instances of things going wrong (much more endearing) than triumphs (why should others take pride in them?).

Parish magazines
Many of these function as local newsletters, and their readership is much wider than just the regular congregation. The editor is usually keen to receive interesting features, and these don't have to be about matters religious. One of my first pieces in print was an article for the parish newsletter on taking part in *Songs of Praise* in St Albans Abbey. As it turned out, there were several publishers in the readership.

Workplace, organisational and club newsletters
Firms, organisations and clubs often produce a regular newsletter to keep up morale and spread information. Taking up (or being told to assume) the editorship can be a poisoned chalice; no one wants to contribute and so you end up writing most of it yourself, or delaying publication because you have little to put in it. If you don't want to

identify yourself as writing for it, give yourself a *nom de plume*, which of course increases interest in your pieces – and your licence to say what you like. When we were stationed in Germany, there was a fascinating column in the garrison magazine written by a 'Camilla Gorse-Bush' on life and gardening; heated discussion took place about who the writer really was, so insightful were her (?) comments.

Reports, summaries and professional correspondence

Report-writing is a chore. But are your reports a pleasure to read? Do you often get feedback from memos or emails you send out? Do you think about the general format before crafting yours, to make them interesting and memorable?

Consider the following from an academic head of department to her staff, encouraging them to come along for their appraisal. It contrasted significantly with the much longer and more bureaucratic memos sent by other academic and support staff.

To: All staff
From: Professor Wendy Lomax, Kingston Business School
Subject: Appraisals

Some of you are avoiding the chance to spend quality time with me in a meeting when you do most of the talking. If you have not yet had your appraisal, please get in touch to make a time.

Professional newsletters

Does your job or profession give you the chance to write? Many professions have a trade magazine or association newsletter. For example, I teach part-time at Kingston University and so have a wonderful opportunity to reach 9,000 alumni, through the newsletter that goes out to them. The editor sent an email appealing for contributions; I wrote a piece, which was printed with a photograph and a special offer on one of my books. As well as yielding a cutting, opportunities like this offer excellent free publicity.

The professional and trade press

Most professions and trades have a formal journal – or indeed several – through which information of interest to that group can be spread. This is an ideal starting point for writers who want to build up a portfolio of cuttings, especially if they plan to write technical and factual books. Such items do not have to be deadly serious. The editor of the *British Dental Journal* once told me that the most widely read column was 'View from the chair' – the humorous end-page, which contrasted with the more serious papers in the rest of the publication.

Writers have several options for writing about writing! See appendix for details.[2]

The local paper

Local papers want local news. It sounds obvious, but if you talk to journalists who work on them they will tell you how much of the potential 'content' provided by those looking for coverage does not meet their requirements. So why not offer to write features and articles as a local writer, or write to the letters page? You will probably not get paid (although it's worth enquiring), but you gain a clipping, and an even more important sense of yourself as a writer, when friends and neighbours read what you have written.

Writing in the knowledge that what you have written may be read by those you see on a daily basis is also, for many budding writers, an important stage in taking themselves seriously. You move from being a closet scribbler to a real writer, and this can boost your self-esteem.

Magazines

Magazines come in a variety of different formats, their unifying characteristics being that they come out at regular intervals and that they want to focus really clearly on their readership – because that is what keeps the readers buying and the advertisers happy. So before thinking about writing for a magazine, buy several copies and study the format. Who is it for, and why would they read it? Is there any pattern you can see in the kind of writing they commission? Do they like 'real life' stories or a more objective analysis of current issues?

Armed with this background, make a list of features you could write and a note of the features editor's email address (usually to

2 *Writers' News, Writing Magazine, Writers Forum, The Bookseller, The Author Magazine* (Society of Authors).

be found in the *Writers' & Artists' Yearbook*). Send an email to find out if you can submit ideas for features, and give them several examples – one punchy paragraph per idea. They will want to see a CV and some examples of your previous writing – which is why it's worth trying to get things published in other places first, so you have something to send.

> "New writers contact me virtually every day with feature ideas. What makes one freelance stand out from another? First, has she emailed? Everyone uses email these days. An old-fashioned letter, especially one with 'First British Serial Rights' on, implying she knows nothing about real journalism, is a no-no.
>
> Second, what is the style and tone of the email? If it's wordy, worthy, plodding, then clearly this writer won't be right for us. If it's bright, snappy, amusing, she might be.
>
> Third, what are the ideas like? Are they fresh, unusual, targeted correctly at the magazine's readership, suggesting she's actually read it?
>
> Fourth, where else has she worked, what are her cuttings like, and her CV? Remember, if a features editor commissions something and it doesn't come up to scratch, it will fall on her, or one of her team, to re-write it. So she's not going to want to take a huge gamble which could turn out to be expensive and time-consuming."
>
> Emma Burstall, Features Editor, *Family Circle*[3]

A word of warning: do make sure you are familiar with the journal before you get in contact. Features editors are not immune to flattery, so commenting on a piece you have seen and enjoyed, and would like to respond to (one that they have commissioned) will probably go down well!

National press
Most features editors on the national press have address books bulging with potential freelance writers. That does not mean to say it is not worth trying to get into print, but you need to follow a few basic rules:

3 For more information, see *Freelance Writing for Newspapers*, Writers' Guides Series, A&C Black (see bibliography).

1 Know the paper you are approaching. Be familiar with the regulars and what has just appeared. Your idea may be great, but if they printed an almost identical piece last week and you don't know about it, you will look a little foolish.

2 Outline your idea clearly, and make reference to wider trends which prove that others are interested. For example, if you want to write about post-natal depression, say how many people suffer from it and if it is a world-wide phenomenon (and if not, perhaps why not). Explain any interesting statistics – is it possible to have PND after other uncomplicated pregnancies?

3 Explain your specific and unique contribution to the process. Why should they commission you rather than taking your idea and giving it to one of their regular writers? Why mustn't they overlook the chance of getting *you* to write it?

4 Don't give them so much of your idea that they either can't wade through it (long emails are hard on the eyes) or you have effectively written the piece for them so they can do it without you.

Celebrity authors – why they get the deals

"Writing is admired these days, admired and envied. Even people who have cast-iron careers in other fields (politicians, movie stars, tennis players) seem to need to write a book, seem to feel driven to leave behind this particular little monument, this testament to the way they thought or spoke – or wish to have been seen to think and speak."

Joanna Trollope, *The Times on Saturday* magazine, 2002

This is an important issue, and one we should deal with early in the book.

Those who really can write, and their supporters, often feel it is grossly unfair that people who have made their name and reputation in a different arena should, once they are famous, be considered prime candidates for publication. The question gets even more vexed when those who are commissioned to write are people who are famous just for being famous – perhaps as a result of a reality television show, attending a lot of parties, or having a comment-worthy (and often surgically enhanced) figure.

There are several reasons why it is in a publisher's interests to commission books by an author who is better known than the product.

In a crowded marketplace, it gets the book noticed

Each year in the UK, 130,000 new books and new editions are published – so it is a huge task to make titles stand out in such a crowded market. Trying to get an unknown author read and stocked in shops is an uphill struggle; a name that already resonates with the public stands a far better chance of getting noticed.

It can bring in valuable revenue

Andy Warhol talked about the enticing prospect of being famous for 15 minutes, and for many people today, celebrity is an obsession. Ask any bunch of teenagers about their plans for the future, and they are likely to reveal that they want to be famous – although they tend to be less concerned about how they are going to achieve fame. The huge sales of celebrity magazines show a widespread fascination with knowing more about the lives of the famous. Books by or about celebrities are part of this trend.

But getting a celebrity book right is *not* an easy equation; it's not an instant path to riches. There are many examples of celebrity non-fiction for which publishers have paid large sums, and which have subsequently flopped.

"Each kind of book – whether it is serious history, literary biography, a sports memoir, commercial women's fiction or a celebrity book – has to be really good of its kind, good enough to succeed in its own right. The key to success is having editors who have a real instinct for what people are going to want to read – and a marketing and sales team who can bring the book to market successfully, with the right cover, title, subtitle, blurb and campaign."

Helen Fraser, Managing Director, Penguin Press

It creates work for ghost writers

The writing of books by celebrities creates opportunities for others to take part in the process – and they are getting better paid and more widely acknowledged for their role. Increasingly, the 'ghosting' of books is becoming less of a spectral profession: some ghost writers now have their role acknowledged on the book cover, in particular for sports biographies, where a sports star may be linked with a like-minded sports journalist.

Ghosting a book is not easy: the writer has to get the voice of the celebrity and produce a convincing and accurate narrative of their lives. This demands real interpretative skills and an ability to get the subject to talk frankly and interestingly – and then to capture their voice. But it is interesting:

> "It's a licence to ask the sort of impertinent questions that you truly want to know the answers to, and to be allowed inside some of the most extraordinary stories. Ghosting makes it quite possible for an unknown author to make a good full-time living as an author; publishers are willing to pay higher advances because they can see how they will market the book once it is written. And once it is written you can move on to your next project; you don't have to do the circuit promoting the book – the star does that themselves (it was their publicity potential that made them 'publishable' in the first place)."
>
> Andrew Crofts

If this interests you, contact the agents listed in the *Writers' & Artists' Yearbook* saying you are available. Bear in mind that the first thing a potential client will want to see is a sample of your work, so be prepared (and read on in this chapter).

It keeps the book on the cultural radar

As long as celebrities and 'media personalities' want to see a book with their name on the cover, the book is promoted as a cultural icon. So even if you would never read a celebrity book yourself, avoid dismissing the genre in general. While some writers confess that they only like reading quality fiction, the truth is that there are vastly more 'general readers', and even more non-readers. It's never a good idea to assume that the rest of the world is as pro-book as you are.

"My son is taking 'A' level English but luckily all the books on the reading list have recently been made into films. So that will save him some time, won't it?"

(Overheard recently)

"One of the most effective ways of engaging reluctant readers, particularly young people, is to expose them to the views and attitudes of their heroes and role models. The involvement of celebrities can have a remarkable impact on prevailing attitudes towards a subject. This is why many literacy projects strive to harness the motivating power of role models from all walks of life, including the famous. These role models inspire people to read by declaring their love of reading, suggesting good reads and often spending time with reluctant readers. The more we can illustrate to people that it is OK to be seen as a reader, the more they will identify with being one."

Stephen Torsi, Reading Champions Project Manager,
National Reading Campaign (National Literacy Trust)

Seeing a famous figure holding a newly published title is surely an important part of ensuring that the book remains within the cultural radar. If celebrities no longer wanted their names on books, I think it would reduce the value of the book as a cultural commodity.

It encourages new readers to come on in

In a recent acceptance speech for the Booker, the author thanked the reader – for without them, there would be no job for writers. Few readers progress straight from the *Oxford Reading Tree* to the complete works of Jane Austen. Many go off reading, either because it is not seen as cool, or because there is too much pressure to complete course work at school – or indeed for a myriad other reasons. Books that are viewed as attractive by emerging readers may tempt them to try others later on. The Reading Agency has done important work in tempting youngsters to read, drawing attention to the sports biography as an enticing start for many young boys:

"It is vital to provide a range of reading materials covering a host of genres in order to help emergent readers develop their reading personalities; time and again people have developed a passion for reading out of their passions in life. There are many examples of boys who, having never before enjoyed a book, suddenly find themselves devouring autobiographies by their favourite footballers, or taking on reads recommended by those that they look up to where previous recommendations from teachers or librarians may have fallen on deaf ears."

Stephen Torsi

Resolve to turn this situation to your advantage

So, instead of carping when the wife of a celebrity is commissioned to write a book for a big advance, think what the publisher's decision tells you about trends in society – and what you can do to ride on the back of them and get your own writing noticed. Could you:

- Write a comment piece for publication, addressing the issues raised (either the subject of the book, or the commission from someone who has never to your knowledge published anything before)?

- Write a letter for publication in a newspaper or magazine about the same thing?

- Try to quantify the interest this reveals in the subject area of the book – and if it is something that has been neglected in the past. Is there room for a second book on the subject?

Summary

Having an established writing portfolio, with real examples of your written work presented for others to enjoy, will increase your confidence, make you hungrier for a more permanent format, and impress a potential publisher or agent. As an example of this in practice, I had written two articles for the *Writers' & Artists' Yearbook* before the publishers of this book offered me a book contract.

Questionnaire

Now turn to the questionnaire at the back of this book and think in detail about your writing and the response you have had from other people. What kind of feedback have you received? How much of a body of circulated/published work, with your name on it, can you present? How much is there that could be put in order, photocopied and sent off to a potential agent or publisher to prove that you can write – and that others want to read what you have written?

Then give yourself a mark out of ten for your effort. If you have not thought of trying to get into print in this way before, leave this section blank and make a firm mental note that you will be more proactive in future. Revisit the questionnaire in six months' time.

3

How creative are you?

Even if your book idea is for an academic monograph of limited circulation, how you format the information you have into a coherent whole is a *creative* decision. You need to consider how the reader can best access your information, in what order they will find it most logically presented, and how to engage their interest. Similarly, the life story of the most compelling and current media star may be told at a plodding pace that repels interest – in which case the photographs had better be good!

For writers of fiction, creativity is crucial. Our desire for the new and the original is moving faster than ever before. The notion of 'time famine' is much quoted, but this is matched with an equally strong desire for the new: new ideas, new stimulation, a new kick:

> "We are more quickly tired of the familiar today. We want something new, but something new that we can connect with."
>
> Ion Trewin, Orion Publishing Group, talking to
> the Society of Authors, September 2005

And maybe this is nothing new:

> "We live at a time when man believes himself fabulously capable of creation, but he does not know what to create."
>
> Jose Ortega y Gasset (1883–1955), Spanish writer and philosopher

So, would-be writers need creativity. They need good ideas that excite others. They need the ability to shape a story, and hold the reader's attention as they do so. But listing creativity as an essential requirement on the writer's CV is one thing; spotting, harnessing and developing it is more difficult.

What is creativity?

"Originality is the essence of the true scholar. Creativity is the soul of the true scholar."

Nnamdi Azikiwe (1904–96), Nigerian President

"The whole point about creative people is that they make stuff up."

Andy Hamilton, *The News Quiz*, BBC Radio 4, 3rd December 2005

It's hard to come up with a definition of creativity; it has many facets, some nebulous, some more concrete. The *New Oxford Dictionary* describes being creative as the 'act of bringing into existence' or 'giving rise to' – although it also includes the definition, 'making a fuss'.

Creativity is often nebulous because it is hard to pin down. All who are in the ideas business agree that they need it, but there is no compensating certainty about what they are looking for:

"We want the thing we don't know about yet. People often ask what we are looking for, but you don't know what you want until someone gives it to you."

Kate Rowland, Creative Director of New Writing at the BBC,
Society of Authors AGM, September 2005

Creativity also works when we are not aware of its operation. The psychoanalyst Jung wrote a lot about creativity, looking at the workings of the unconscious. Whether this is innate or can be developed is a matter of speculation. The poet Samuel Taylor Coleridge commented:

"There are two kinds of imagination, primary and secondary. We all possess the primary imagination, we all have the capacity to perceive and to notice. But what only poets (for this read 'creative people') have, the secondary imagination, is the capacity to select, and then to translate and illuminate, everything that has been observed so that it seems to the audience something entirely new, something entirely true, something excitingly wonderful or terrible."

Biographia Literaria

Aristotle talks about the creative mind making connections between things, and psychiatrists Jackson and Messick have talked about the importance of novelty to creativity; the creative person's ability to transform and condense existing ideas and put them together in new combinations. Others agree:

> "The creative act is essentially integrative. Opposites are united; disparate elements are reconciled."
>
> Antony Storr, *Churchill's Black Dog*, quoted in
> Julia Casterton's *Creative Writing* (see bibliography)

A key quality of the creative mind is the refining one, making a new something out of things that already exist, spotting a pattern and taking it on to its next logical stage; an ability to make something out of nothing. In *The Act of Creation*, Arthur Koestler identifies:

> "... that essential element of the creative as the combination of previously unrelated items of experience, whether mental or physical. It is precisely one's recognition of patterns of relationship previously ignored by others that serves as a basis of this 'discovery' of the new, different or novel product under investigation. And this cognitive ability is none other than the innate mental function of intuition described by Jung."

Or more prosaically:

> "Creativeness often consists in turning up what is already there. Did you know that left and right shoes were thought up only a little more than a century ago?"
>
> Bernice Fitz-Gibbon (1895–1982), US advertising executive

Creativity can include simplifying, and progressive work of many artists demonstrates this process. Henry Moore's sculptures, Picasso's line drawings and Matisse's reliefs all get simpler – and stronger – as time progresses:

> "Technical skill is mastery of complexity while creativity is mastery of simplicity."
>
> EC Zeeman (b1923), British mathematician

Creativity can also be more substantial. Liz Attenborough, former Managing Director of Puffin (the children's imprint of Penguin), described creativity as 'a thing' because you can feel yourself putting it to one side to do later, or to do after some displacement activity – and anything that can be shifted must exist in a real form.

Creative idea or copy?

How do you distinguish between something that is original and something that is derivative – i.e. based on the success of an idea originally developed by someone else? Is there a hierarchy of creativity? Is the creativity displayed in a classic novel greater than the creativity of a wrestler's moves in the ring? Does pleasure in an item that is derivative mean it is a lesser pleasure? Is preferring the novels of a modern romantic novelist to those of Jane Austen a judgemental choice or just personal preference?

The important thing is for you, the writer, to be completely clear as to whether or not you are being derivative. There is nothing wrong with using other influences in your work – indeed, the best writers often do – as long as you are honest about it. Take a long objective look at your work; perhaps show it to others for confirmation; be sure to give credit where it is due.

Creativity today

Creative Writing courses are booming today in schools and colleges. At the same time, there are trainers working in industry to boost staff creativity – on the grounds that if we feel free to invent and think around a subject, both our effectiveness at work and our personal happiness will be enhanced. For many, it's a question of trying to feel creative again, trying to go back to the instinctive creativity that we were encouraged to develop in the school classroom:

> "Creative imagination awakens early. As children we are all 'makers'. Later, as a rule, we're broken of the habit; so the art of

being a creative writer consists, among other things, in not allowing life or people or money to turn us aside from it."

Stig Dagerman (1923–54), Swedish writer

As author Livi Michael pointed out to me, in junior school we write a story a week – but in secondary school this becomes a much more serious 'essay'.

Often, courses in creativity are based on trying to stimulate the brain into sparking. They encourage us to put familiar ideas into new combinations, or to think through concepts that would previously have been considered unsuitable – 'thinking the unthinkable'.

There are also fashions in creativity:

"Before the Renaissance, writers and artists were valued for their skills rather than their individuality. Today the originality of creative writers, whether they be novelists, playwrights or poets, is inescapably linked with self-exploration. The writing we most value is that which makes an authentic, individual statement; which conveys the writer's personal view of life."

Anthony Storr, writing on depression in *The Author* magazine

In some areas of artistic endeavour, what is described as 'creative' is what can shock us most, either by its radical nature or by the number of noughts after the price tag next to it. So the latest art offering by a wild child artist gets discussed according to how much it costs and the news value it offers, rather than whether or not the idea is intrinsically interesting – as indeed many of them are.

To take just one example, the actress Tilda Swinton lying inside a glass box and allowing the public to watch her sleep was a really interesting idea, and one which drew crowds when the installation was displayed at the Serpentine Gallery as part of an exhibition by Cornelia Parker. The chance to look at another human being really close up is rare in today's society, and to see someone else asleep is a real intimacy – as those who suddenly wake up on the train, having fallen asleep between stations, often realise (they are usually embarrassed and then look around quickly to see who else has noticed they were asleep). A discussion of the event merely in terms of what it cost to stage diminished the genuine creativity it encompassed.

The same can happen in publishing. An event can occur which captures the public's imagination, but if it is handled with creativity and imagination, this will ensure that it embeds itself deeper in the public consciousness. So a shocking story of a murder becomes ingrained in our imagination the more detail we learn, and the more we come to identify with the protagonists. The creative writer doesn't just describe events; he or she draws us into the basic framework, adding key details of character, background and plot to involve us further. It's the difference between a scene-of-crime report compiled by the police, and a good 'whodunnit'.

How creative are you?

Here are six quick exercises

1 How many smaller words can you create out of the word 'encyclopaedia'?

2 How many uses can you think of for a flowerpot?

3 Imagine the building you are sitting in right now, but upside-down. How would you get from the top to the bottom? What would happen to the cupboards? How would you get in?

4 How many times today have you made a creative decision?

5 Consider the following items: a metal bedstead, a broken coat-hanger, three bottles of beer, a fire-alarm sounding, a dog barking. What is going on? Whose room is this and what has just happened? Who is there?

6 Go to the dampest place in your home or place of work (this may be the garage, a deep cupboard, or the basement). Inhale deeply and then imagine what individual elements make up the smell. Try to list all the constituent parts, and to write them down as quickly as possible.

Feedback on the exercises
Exercise 1
The creative mind starts spotting the obvious choices and then develops strategies for how to find more (first letter and second, first letter and third, first letter and fourth, etc.).

Exercise 2
The creative mind will find many alternative uses that are not immediately apparent – such as a hat, a stepping stone, a strengthened fist, etc. It will also tend to redefine the question, thus asking whether it is a plastic or terracotta flowerpot, and of what size?

Exercise 3
The creative mind will not be put off by the apparent illogicality of the scenario suggested, and will work away at coming to understand the new arrangements. It will also spot some interesting side-effects (the white ceilings would quickly get dirty as people walked on them).

Exercise 4
Whereas the initial response may be not even once, the creative mind will look for opportunities where some creativity was exercised – such as what to wear, which mug to choose for a drink, how to arrange toast on a plate, and what kind of route to take to work.

Exercise 5
The creative mind relishes this kind of challenge; it will engage and come up with a response to how these disparate items are connected. What is more, their imagined union will quickly seem so real that the individual will come to believe the linkage really happened.

Exercise 6
Our sense of smell is often much more acute than we realise; most of us take it for granted. And if you concentrate and write quickly, accessing a flow of consciousness, you will probably be surprised by how much emerges from casual observation.

In response to all these exercises, the creative mind will go on working on the problems set, whether consciously or subconsciously, long after the timeframe has elapsed.

Nurturing your creativity

"Cultivate your own 'acre of ground' – all the things that made you the person you are: your family, childhood, locality, religion, friends, lovers, influences and experiences. This is the basis of your writing material and should prove very fertile. Carry a notebook at all times. Makes notes on the weather, on weddings, funerals, or family gatherings, on the people you see on buses, trains or planes. Get into the habit of listening and observing.

All locations and experiences can yield creative fruit; it's the writer's attitude that matters. He or she needs to be constantly observing and listening, antennae out, to pick up the seeds of a story. Even the smallest thing can be turned into fiction. We need to replace our blindness with a habit of total openness to people, nature, conversations, and so on. Vivid details bring truth and vibrancy to writing, so we need to observe the details of skies, birds, flowers, people's faces, etc. We need to poke around in rubbish bins, look at rivers at different times and seasons, listen to how people speak – the things they don't say – the silences, the implications. Writers are never on holiday.

Build up an image bank, like an artist or photographer. Also keep a daily journal, recording any interesting thoughts or incidents, or any strong or complex emotions. The journal is your 'larder' stocked with fodder for your future writing."

Wendy Perriam

"For an author, any activity which isn't writing – like changing a toilet roll, tidying a sock drawer, phoning an editor, or sleeping – is displacement activity. I think most of my work is done during displacement activities, particularly sleep."

Nicholas Allan

In the same way that you are attuned to what makes you creative, keep away from things that make you feel blocked – whether substances, people or opinions.

"I find ignorance particularly soul-destroying. My work seems to have taken me to places that are politically oppressive. Seeing people blinded by political propaganda is close to unbearable. This includes working in Britain of course. I can feel very miserable when someone has behaved ignorantly or expressed ignorant opinions."

Edward Denison

"Don't block your creativity with drink, drugs, junk food, endless busyness or harmful relationships."

Wendy Perriam

"Some friends are excellent for you as a writer who are worthless to you otherwise – and vice versa … If you feel, after an evening with the stolid friend, that the world is a dry and dusty place, or if you are exasperated to the point of speechlessness by your brilliant acquaintance, not the warmest emotion for them will justify your seeing much of them while you are trying to learn to write … You will have to find other acquaintances, persons who, for some mysterious reason, leave you full of energy, feed you with ideas, or more obscurely still, have the effect of filling you with self-confidence and eagerness to write."

Dorothea Brande (see bibliography)

Ten top tips on how to nurture your creativity

1 **Read a lot**, in lots of different formats (see chapter 9). Try to read publications you do not agree with, or would not habitually buy, as well as those that confirm your own viewpoint.

2 **Daydream**. About anything, whenever you can. For example, think of a character whose job you have never considered in great detail – perhaps a bank teller or a school caretaker – and imagine yourself into their daily life. Gaze into someone else's shopping trolley at the supermarket checkout and imagine the lifestyle that goes with it.

"Most persons who are attracted by the idea of fiction at all are, or were in childhood, great dreamers."

Dorothea Brande (see bibliography)

3 **Make time for yourself.** The creative person often needs time and space in their brain for ideas to develop.

"It is necessary to be slightly under-employed if you want to do something significant."

James Dewey Watson (b1928), US biochemist

Interestingly, a recent study of children by a team from London University found that the more activities children are involved in, the less creative they feel[1] – an antidote to the modern parent's desire to fill their child's time with activities, on the grounds that they are stimulating them and giving them 'a head start'.

4 **Lead an interesting life.** Do the unexpected; visit exhibitions you know nothing about, see plays and films that would not have been your first choice, and then analyse what you saw. Take part!

For example, through a friend of a friend, I once went to the preview of a Barry Manilow musical and found myself in a complete world of similar-looking women, all of whom responded in the same way to the composer's sudden – and unexpected – appearance. *En masse*, they sighed. I thought the musical was good (and it was interesting to compare the strong feelings the composer's name arouses with the work he produces), but I was as intrigued by the audience's behaviour as I was by the spectacle on the stage.

5 **Keep up with trends in your artistic area.** Know what has been written and what is in development. Have your own ideas about how such projects could be tackled.

6 **Recognise that there are times of the day when you feel more creative than others** – and that these are different for different people. I find my brain often produces ideas at 2.00 a.m., so have

1 Reported in *The Daily Telegraph*, 29th October 2005.

learnt to keep a notepad by my bed. If the idea is really persistent I go upstairs to my computer and write a few paragraphs down, the silence of the house around me making the effort more special:

"I imagine this midnight moment's forest
Something else is alive
Beside the clock's loneliness
And this blank page where my fingers move."

Ted Hughes (1930–98), writer and poet, from *The Thought Fox*

Others find early morning best, or lunchtime, or in the car or the bathroom. Whatever works for you, try to see this as part of your inspiration rather than something that must be subjugated to domestic rhythms – although obviously, finding your writing habit in full flow at 8.00 a.m. can be a little difficult if you have to get children off to school. If this is the case, promise yourself that you will get started as soon as they are away, and tell them what you are doing – this will help your sense of yourself as a writer. Let others know too what works best for you – a friend of mine has let us know that from 9.00 until 12.00 she is writing, and we all respect this.

7 **Learn something new** – take up an evening class, an Open University course or a summer school. If you are used to using your brain in an analytical way all day, employing it in a different way later in the day can be very effective, for example by taking up pottery or flower arranging. Mowing the lawn or hanging out the washing can be very soothing and can give your brain a chance to come up with new ideas if you have been writing all day.

8 **Listen to something new.** If you normally listen to Radio 4, try the commercial radio stations; if you are a Radio 1 fan, try Radio 3 for a change. If you usually travel with your own music source through headphones, switch it off and listen to other people's conversations or opinions. Conversations overheard on buses are particularly fruitful!

9 If time and income permit, **take on a job that requires a different kind of attention** from your usual type of work. For example, if your job is desk-based or pressurised, could you volunteer to help in a

school, hearing children read, or to help out in a charity shop? A new and often tight-set list of workplace rules and a different vocabulary may give you the freedom to think in a new way, and inspire further creativity. One first-time novelist recently talked about the beneficial effects of a low-grade civil service job, which gave her the energy for thinking about her writing; a GP I know took a cabin crew job with an airline and found that it released huge reserves of energy in her. The poet Philip Larkin worked in the library at Hull University.

"The more we reduce ourselves to machines in the lower things, the more force we shall set free to use in the higher."

Anna C Brackett (1836–1911), US writer

10 **Have opinions.** Being opinionated is often seen as a negative trait, but writers need opinions; they need to feel strongly in order to write convincingly. Ensure that you expose yourself to lots of different opinions, not just those you agree with. Consider joining a discussion group (perhaps online) and maintain links with a wide variety of people.

"Contradictions, if well understood and managed, can spark off the fires of invention. Orthodoxy whether of the right or of the left is the graveyard of creativity."

Chinua Achebe (b1930), Nigerian novelist and poet

"Perhaps some of my hearers may occasionally have heard it stated of me that I am rather apt to contradict myself. I hope that I am exceedingly apt to do so. I have never met with a question yet, of any importance, which did not need, for the right solution of it, at least one positive and one negative answer."

John Ruskin (1819–1900), British art critic, writer and reformer

Physical circumstances that help you feel more creative

Most budding writers are fascinated by the working practices of those who have made it into print (see chapter 5 for more information on this).

Sometimes, changing your physical circumstances can give your creativity a boost. The following list was compiled as a result of detailed discussions with lots of writers, who feel creative through:

"Giving myself a time limit. When I first started writing, I only had an hour a day, and that only when my husband was home from the sea. (I had small children and no grandparents near.) I didn't waste a second of that hour because I had been planning what to write in it all day. I meet writers who suddenly have 'time to write' who feel incredibly guilty about not spending all day writing. Some of them can't even start. I tell them to limit the amount of writing time to an hour, or even half an hour. I think it helps!"

Katie Fforde

"A devotedly dull and routine life, with as little excitement and change, is the best thing by far."

Philip Pullman

"I find smells make me feel creative. In my writing room I often have some essential oils warming (Bergamot is particularly stimulating), and I buy exotic hand-creams to rub on when my brain needs a boost."

"Trying to create some distance from my research and previous thinking, allowing that to be background and letting the front of my brain do the writing. I have developed the habit of doing all the research and thinking from my desk, but then going somewhere completely neutral to do the writing. Once installed, I like as little interruption as possible; I do not want to be brought coffee and I do not have access to email or a telephone. I like to think that when I am operating like this I am a helicopter, hovering above my subject, observing the shape of the landscape and the long-term direction and not bogged down in the intricacies of the research that fuelled it. Once I am down from this broad drafting I will check back against my notes, but the creative process is essentially hovering above rather than nitty-gritty."

"Research is an incredibly helpful displacement activity. I'm usually doing some kind of research both before and in tandem with the writing, on each novel. For *Mr Wroe's Virgins* and *Promised Lands* I found it helpful to immerse myself in original material (journals and letters) from the period. This was partly for the flavour of the language but also for details which then found their way into the novel – or, indeed, inspired changes and connections in the novel. So early colonists' descriptions of Australian wildlife in terms of English animals (the kangaroo is a rabbit crossed with a deer) gave me an insight into the grid they carried in their own heads: initially the new world could only be experienced and explained in terms of the old, because they lacked any other way of seeing it. For *Island* I researched Celtic fairy tales, and the history of the Hebrides; for *The Voyage Home*, Ibo culture. When I am stuck with the writing I turn back to research, and find it usually sets me thinking again."

Jane Rogers

"Coffee and chocolate, in that order."

"Coffee, a brisk walk, and turn off the Internet. I also make sound-tracks for my books – music that reflects the mood or ideas in my story. Listening to the soundtrack puts me in the right state of mind to work. Walking makes my ideas flow more easily. Taking a bath helps too."

Julie Cohen

"Watching soaps on television. I find them so absorbing, I totally relax."

"For a sense of what makes a good narrative structure and style I think watching TV soaps and drama is good. It's important, as a writer, to have a good sense of contemporary media language."

Sheila Cornelius

"Ironing. Polishing. Gardening. Something with an instant reward that still requires concentration to leave your right brain free to work imaginatively. The sea always makes me feel creative, as do trees at night, Baroque music and firelight. I also wear different scents when

I'm writing about different characters. A very complicated, private, competent career woman in the 1940s gets Bulgari 'Green Tea', for example."

Jenny Haddon

"Bookshops make me feel creative. Read what other people have written. You will either feel inspired or think to yourself, 'I could do that and I could do it better!'."

Adam Powley

"Taking public transport. I find the lack of responsibility (someone else is driving) and the ability to just look out of the window helps me put my mind into neutral and I often have some really good ideas. The mental vacuum of staring out of the window is supported by just a touch of tension (will we be on time?) to enable me to be creative. Once I was driving a hire car because ours was being repaired. I could not work out how to use the radio, and had not brought a tape with me. It turned out to be a really creative journey as I just concentrated on the driving and my mind was in free-flow. I had some really good ideas that day!"

"Being driven by someone else who does not insist on talking but takes me through an unfamiliar route. There's something about rejoining familiar streets from unfamiliar angles that often prompts really good ideas."

"Standing in my bare feet on grass. I know the benefits of reflex-ology are well established – massaging parts of your feet has been shown to loosen up your entire body - but there's something about the feel of grass on my feet that refreshes me all the way through."

"Going out with the smokers for a gossip. Because I can really forget what I was thinking about before that point. The same goes for reading *Hello* magazine, it is so absorbing you cannot think of anything else at the same time, and that is why one feels totally relaxed afterwards."

"Swimming or running. I find it difficult to think and exercise at the same time, and so this really does give my brain a rest. Even better when I can run and tune into daytime television, which is absorbing without being unduly demanding. When I go back to writing afterwards I always feel a greater enthusiasm."

"A hot bath with lots of smelly ingredients, low lights and calm music."

"Going for a walk with an artist. I studied art history at university and I remember a lecturer recommending that you go for a walk looking at the scenery through the eyes of a favourite artist. It's still one of my favourite ways of relaxing, half closing my eyes to get the full picture."

"Tidying up. I find putting my papers in order and tidying my desk is a great way of preparing to write."

"Chaos. I like to write in the middle of a mess. It makes me concentrate on the smooth lines of what I am writing, and emerges in a pleasing order."

"I have great belief in the fact that whenever there is chaos, it creates wonderful thinking. I consider chaos a gift."

Septima Poinsette Clark (1898–1987), US educator

"My office is chaotic and colourful – rather like myself – and has a tendency to get very untidy – also like me. The first thing I do when settling down to some serious work is to create order in the chaos. It doesn't take long, as most of the jumble is in layers rather like strata that reflect the time since I last tidied.

Then once I'm clear I usually go somewhere else and curl up with a pad and pencil. I'm a visual thinker and need first of all to create a mind map of what I want to do. Sometimes I draw endless spider diagrams branching off all over the place; at other times, boxes and odd shapes connected by lines and arrows appear. This usually reaches a peak where everything seems unmanageable until I have a flash of inspiration and it becomes in some way ordered. Then I'm ready to go back and get on with it."

Gill Hines

"I need an 'external' deadline or it never gets done, i.e. someone asking for a piece of work by a given date or time. I then write, right up to the deadline, through the night sometimes if necessary. But otherwise it never gets done."

Stephen Hancocks

"Giving yourself a break from words. The 'Big Brother' household allows no paper and pencils or anything to read – which would make me long to write."

"If you stop reading you get desperate and start reading adverts and computer instruction manuals. It makes you write stories because you're deprived of reading them."

Nicholas Allan

What does creativity feel like?

Creativity may be hard to define, but some writers I spoke to could definitely recognise its onset. Others could only spot it in retrospect, looking back on what they had written the day or year before, and identifying a quality of thought or style there.

"I have that continuous uncomfortable feeling of 'things' in the head, like icebergs or rocks or awkwardly placed pieces of furniture. It's as if all the nouns were there but the verbs were lacking."
Elizabeth Bishop (1911–79), US poet, referring to the difficulties of writing

Sometimes, ideas come quickly:

"I have learnt to recognise the feeling that a great idea is coming. I can feel this sort of buzzing in my ears and then it seems to just flow through my fingers, like a projectile vomit. The feeling may last for just 15 minutes but feel like hours. Afterwards I feel utterly sated."

"Those first songs I wrote, I was just taking notes at a fantastic rock concert that was going on inside my head."
Jim Morrison (1943–71), US rock singer and songwriter

"Like a quiet explosion in your head."

Maurice Sendak (b1928), US illustrator and author

"The great jazz giants whom I have heard … have all made the same striking impression that, were the instrument to be suddenly wrenched from their lips, the music would continue to flow out of sheer creative momentum."

Humphrey Lyttleton (b1921), British Jazz trumpeter

"Just now I've taen the fit o' rhyme
My barmie noddle's working prime."

Robert Burns, *The Epistle to James Smith*

Several writers talked about the importance of acknowledging your really creative ideas; of sitting back and being impressed by what has just popped into your head. Philip Pullman had already written several versions of the opening version of *Northern Lights* when he hit on the idea of characters having 'daemons' who represent their characters:

"It was the realisation that each character had a daemon, a sort of personification of part of themselves in animal form, that led me into the story in the first place; but there was still something wrong with it. I knew that if that was all it consisted of, readers would soon get weary of it. It was only when – after a long period of thinking about it – I realised that there was a difference between children's daemons and those of adults, namely that children's daemons could change form whereas adults' were fixed, that I found the key to the whole book. And that was enormously exciting."

But where did the idea suddenly come from? Of course, ideas that appear suddenly are usually the result of prior – albeit unconscious – preparation; of drawing on months of careful thinking and reading. Thus the essential simplicity of late Picasso line drawings is born of a lifetime of artistic practice. But the arrival of an important idea is tremendously exciting and needs to be acknowledged. Dorothea Brande quotes FWH Myers' concept of 'subliminal uprush' (from the chapter on 'Genius' in his *Human*

Personality, and further comments: "If you are to write well, you must come to terms with the enormous and powerful part of your nature which lies behind the threshold of immediate knowledge." Others have described this as an 'artistic coma', out of which good ideas come, and Stephen King has referred to stories 'simmering away in that place that's not quite the conscious but not quite the subconscious, either' and the moment at which everything connects as 'thinking above the curve' or 'over-logic':

"There is no Idea Dump, no Story Central, no Island of the Buried Bestsellers; good story ideas seem to come quite literally from nowhere, sailing at you right out of the empty sky: two previously unrelated ideas come together and make something new under the sun. Your job isn't to find these ideas but to recognise them when they show up."

Sometimes, though, creativity is a struggle. This notion – of creativity coming out of struggle – is long established:

"Creation comes out more beautiful from a form rebellious to work: verse, marble, onyx or enamel."

Theophile Gautier (1811–72), French poet and critic

"I do not believe in the kind of art which has not forced its way out through man's need to open his heart – all art, literature as well as music, must be created with one's heart's blood."

Edvard Munch (1863–1944), Norwegian artist

"I've found that location, different experiences, people, are of no help whatsoever to jump-starting creativity. Creativity comes mainly from boredom and anger. I sit at a table for about five hours a day with a pen and paper. I soon get bored, and in the end, angry."

Nicholas Allan

An important point for writers to spot is when, even though they may be conscious of the need to maintain the practice of writing – or what advertising executive Bill Bernbach (1911–82) called 'properly practised creativity' – there is just no spark. For most writers in this situation, the best thing is to give yourself a break. Stopping in the middle of a piece of writing and having a break can often keep me going for much longer than if I stick at it all day without proper rests. It's taken me a while to realise that time is largely immaterial to the quality of what I produce. Sometimes I can produce in 15 minutes what at other times might take me three hours to write. It all depends on how it is going.

And for some, the creative process remains a mystery, best not examined:

"It's like driving a car at night. You never see further than your headlights, but you can make the whole trip that way."
EL Doctorow (b1931), US novelist – referring to his own creative technique

"I myself would be hard pressed if I had to decide who had written what I write. I accept no responsibility for the writing process; but I can vouch for the accuracy of what is depicted."
Benito Perez Galdos (1843–1920), Spanish novelist and playwright

Summary

Ultimately, a writer's creativity is what keeps us interested in reading their work. It can work on many levels – the elegant combination of prose and subject, the satisfying neatness of the workings-out of a novel, the twist of a piece of detective fiction, the unravelling of a life through a well-researched and well-written biography, a greater understanding on the part of the reader about their own self, reached through reading about the imagined lives of others. And it is a vital asset for any would-be writer, for:

"Creation comes before distribution – or there will be nothing to distribute."
Ayn Rand (1905–82), Russian-born writer and philosopher

Questionnaire

Look back through this chapter and think about your own level of creativity. Does what you write spark a response from those you show it to? Are they interested in knowing what will happen next? Do you have unusual ideas, get delight from putting people and places into mixed contexts?

Give yourself a mark out of ten for how creative you think you are. As with all these tick-boxes, there is the chance to review your score in a few months' time, once you have worked on the various creativity-boosting exercises provided. For now, be honest about your *current* level of creativity.

4

What are your personal support mechanisms like?

"Creating is a harrowing business. I work in a state of anguish all year. I shut myself up, I don't go out. It's a hard life, which is why I understand Proust so well; I have such an admiration for what he has written about the agony of creation."

Yves Saint Laurent (b1936), couturier

Let's be honest here, living with a writer is not easy. And whereas living with a published writer is no picnic – all those highs and lows, each new project bringing with it a new set of research obsessions and deadlines, the constant fear that you will not be able to do it all again – living with someone who aspires to write can be even harder. They are trying to support their dream; you are trying to support them.

Writing – a very ordinary talent?

I touched on this problem in chapter 1. Writing is seen by many as an obvious talent; indeed, its branding as a 'life skill' is hardly helpful to the professional writer. Despite concerns over literacy levels in schools, most of us emerged from the educational process able to string a sentence together and to write it down. And stories in the press of people making it as writers very quickly have enhanced the impression that writing is easy, and a swift path to riches.

Just as pleasant or interesting jobs tend to pay badly (ski-repping, publishing, working in an art gallery or for a wine merchant), so anything that is on the school curriculum but can be turned into an occupation seems to draw cynicism. Writing, painting, teaching sport, acting and other creative arts tend to attract the accusation that the protagonists have not fully grown up; that you are indulging a habit you should really have grown out of by now.

But while not allowing life or people or money to turn us aside is fine in theory, the practical living part of this can be more difficult. Writers are easily bruised; few publicly announce their intention to get published straight off, since it feels like tempting fate. And even those who have several books to their name may claim that they do something else rather than submit to the following, and oft re-enacted, conversation:

Question:	What do you do?
Writer:	I write.[1]
Question:	Have you had anything published?
Writer:	Well yes actually, it's x (name of your book).
Questioner:	I've never heard of it.

Most writers have suffered with a string of personal put-downs, which the authors I consulted were quick to share with me:

- "How long does it take you to churn one out?"
- "Why do you bother? There are too many books in the world anyway."
- "So, how would you respond to those people who say that the sort of books you write are aimed at housewives who're not very well educated?"
- "You're somewhere between commercial and literary, and that's always a problem."
- "I wrote a book once and never got anywhere. And so and so wrote two novels which also came to nothing. Of course you might have more success. Have you thought of self-publishing?"
- "If it's not about David Beckham or Man U, we don't want to know."

---

1 And that's assuming that you resist the temptation to hop from foot to foot and say, 'I am trying to write.'

And unpublished authors who write in another format (normally journalists who plan to write a book, once they have the time), can be even more dismissive:

> "An awful lot of authors get published because they're producing the sort of formulaic stuff that publishers want, while so many of the rest of us are simply too quirky and original to get published."[2]

The trouble is that while all the above will have a resonance for other writers, the rest of the world may be less sympathetic, thinking us fragile and in need of coddling. In reality, the writer needs a strong ego – a strong sense of self, and of self as a writer – in order to work at all. Writing a book for publication is, after all, an intensely egotistical act, based as it is on the premise that your viewpoint should be read and appreciated by others.

> "I am still writing. I have just finished my third novel and I am going to go on writing because I refuse to believe that I won't be published. I've come to understand that the arrogance is an essential part of self-belief. I have to feel my work is exceptional because otherwise I would not be excited enough to write. Also I feel as if I am nearly there. One more push, one more novel, one acceptance. And my family are terrific."
>
> John Whitley

> "No, I don't think I am arrogant, I think I am riddled with too much self-doubt. I think a lot of the problem with me goes back to being an indulged only child. Anyone who sits down and writes a 100,000-word novel thinks that what they've got to say is quite important."
>
> Tony Parsons, *Sunday Telegraph*, 28th August 2005

> "A good stylist should have a narcissistic enjoyment as he works. He must be able to objectivise his work to such an extent that he catches himself feeling envious ... In short, he must display that highest degree of objectivity which the world calls vanity."
>
> Karl Kraus (1874–1936), Austrian writer

---

2 Quoted in Maggie Craig's excellent piece 'Pick a window, pal', *The Author*, Summer 2005.

Large egos get tolerated in small doses, and particularly if they make a lot of money. Large egos in a smaller environment, where space is limited and money tight, can be less welcome.

Top tips for supporting your desire to write

Support from family

While encouragement is often helpful to the budding writer, the family response does not have to be positive. Many books have been written in a spirit of 'I'll show them' or as a result of dogged determination in the face of hostility, as in the case of Flora Thompson (*Lark Rise*, etc.). I admit that my unborn son was the motivation for my first book. From the moment I announced I was pregnant, I got so fed up with people looking me in the stomach rather than in the face, and being generally talked down to in clinics, that I became determined to use my brain too. And the unmoveable deadline is immensely useful: I finished the book shortly before he was born.

"Most writers do well with family support. It helps if money is not a problem. On the other hand, I've written some of my best work through very harrowing times, so there's no hard and fast rule. If life is too cosy and comfortable there's a danger that our writing gets slack; I find that difficult times make me work harder at my writing."

Sharon Maas

"My wife made a crucial difference during those two years I spent teaching at Hampden (and washing sheets at New Franklin Laundry during the summer vacation). If she had suggested that the time I spent writing stories on the front porch of our rented house on Pond Street or in the laundry room of our rented trailer on Klatt Road in Hermon was wasted time, I think a lot of the heart would have gone out of me. Tabby never voiced a single doubt, however. Her support was constant, one of the few good things I could take as a given. And whenever I see a first novel dedicated to a wife (or a husband), I smile and think, there's someone who knows. Writing is a lonely job. Having someone who believes in you makes a lot of difference."

Stephen King, *On Writing* (see bibliography)

"I think it is helpful to live with someone who at least respects your right to choose how you spend your time, and who respects writing because they like reading. Self-confidence helps, too, but that is reinforced, for me, by reading about writers."

Sheila Cornelius

Ironically, those you might expect most encouragement from can be slow in delivering up the goods. Family and older friends can be much less ready to acknowledge what you have achieved, simply because they have known you for much longer, and so remember you as a scabby-kneed eight-year-old.

"My relatives and friends told me I was wasting my time trying to write, let alone make a living out of it. I always believed them, but was stubborn enough to want to find out for myself. I was surprised to find they were wrong. The only real emotional support for a writer is to see his or her work stay in print."

Nicholas Allan

They may also inherently disapprove of the fact that you are choosing to write at all:

"I don't come from an educated family and my sisters positively condemn my involvement with writing because it distracts me from more traditional female pursuits such as being preoccupied with house and family."

Sheila Cornelius

"A writer needs family and friends who don't think you're wasting their time. Ditto who don't mind you shunning them when you're on a writing roll. Ditto who don't mind if you don't show them your work – you have to pick your critics so carefully! Ditto who even then don't mind you crying on their shoulder. What worked best for me was my husband leaving. It has many disadvantages, but I do get every other weekend completely child-free to write in, and usually a fortnight in the summer."

Emma Darwin

Support from friends

Most of us have different sorts of friends. Some you go for out-door walks with; others you meet while shopping or link up with for a drink in a wine bar. Sometimes – most often at 'big birthday' parties – the various groups overlap.

Writers need friends of various sorts. The kind who will give you objective advice on what you have written, and pragmatic advice on what to do next, are of course very useful, but I think most writers would credit the real balm for the soul to those friends who are just dead impressed that you are trying to write, and even more so if you get anything published.

For example, I sent my friend Harriet Carrow a copy of my most recent book, together with a few of the leaflets the publishers had produced to mark publication. When I rang her to find out what she thought, she said she had the book in her kitchen (the most frequently used room in the house) and had displayed the title in her cookery-book reading-stand, with a pile of leaflets next to it. She said she had shown the book to all callers and handed out leaflets to many. What is more, she gave me the distinct impression that she was pleased to be doing this – she said she felt proud to know a 'real writer'. I can't tell you what this did for my morale.

"I say to kind friends and relatives whom I've asked to take a look at my efforts – 'constructive criticism only, please'. Anything too harsh could put me off completely! I'm that sensitive! But constructive suggestions can really help. It's all in the way you say it, I guess!"

Emma Burstall

"If you are writing alone, having someone you who know can offer an honest and constructive opinion is key. The support of family, friends and colleagues was also a big help for me."

Adam Powley

"A writer needs someone to talk to about their work who under-stands about work in progress and won't sit in judgement too early or offer intrusive suggestions. That someone should not be involved in your professional writing life or your personal life, both of which introduce incompatible stresses in other directions."

Jenny Haddon

> "Some friends are excellent for you as a writer who are worthless to
> you otherwise – and vice versa ... If you feel, after an evening with
> the stolid friend, that the world is a dry and dusty place, or if you are
> exasperated to the point of speechlessness by your brilliant acquain-
> tance, not the warmest emotion for them will justify your seeing
> much of them while you are trying to learn to write ... You will have
> to find other acquaintances, persons who, for some mysterious
> reason, leave you full of energy, feed you with ideas, or more
> obscurely still, have the effect of filling you with self-confidence and
> eagerness to write."
>
> Dorothea Brande (see bibliography)

Along similar lines, here is the advice given to a close friend by her
doctor, who had recently diagnosed a terminal illness. It's excellent advice for the living as well as for the sick:

> "If people upset you, and their presence continues in an unwelcome
> fashion in your head long after they have left, don't feel you've got
> to carry on seeing them just because you have known them for a
> long time. Make the best use of your time; you have no obligation to
> make equal access of yourself to everyone."

Who wants you to write a book?

It's worth considering just whose idea is it that you should write a
book. It's not uncommon for creative people, or those who would
feel fulfilled by living with/being married to a writer, to push their
ambitions onto a third party. Consider the following comments
from Noel Coward, writing about his long-time companion,
Graham Payn:

> "He is, I fear, a born drifter. I know his theatrical career has been a
> failure but there are other ploys to go after. He sleeps and sleeps
> and the days go by. I love him dearly for ever ... and am happy to
> look after him for the rest of my life, but he must do something.
> If only he would take up some occupation and stick to it. I know
> that he is unhappy inside but, alas, with his natural resilience these

moments of self-revelation dissipate and on go the years and he will be an elderly man who has achieved nothing at all.

He has had so many chances and failed. He knows this of course and I am sure that he has many miserable moments, but he won't work unless he has to – then he is at it like a tiger – but he lacks the self-discipline to force himself. He hasn't pressed on with learning to type. He reads only trash and that very seldom."

What comes over is Coward's intellectual restlessness at his friend's indolence. In fact, after Coward's death in Jamaica in 1973, Payn collaborated with Sheridan Morley and Cole Lesley on *Noel Coward and his Friends* (1979); after Lesley's death in 1980 he edited, with Morley, *The Noel Coward Diaries* (1982), which the pair dedicated to Cole Lesley. He continued to administrate Coward's estate from the playwright's house in Switzerland.[3]

Quick quiz

Writers need different kind of friends for different sorts of news. Who would you turn to if:

* You received a rejection from a publisher or agent, having been given very positive feedback up to this point?
* Your book has just been chosen for a WH Smith promotion?
* Your publisher has suggested severe amendments to the manuscript you have been working on for years, and you are now in danger of not meeting the publication date?

Ironically, you are just as much in need of friends once you are successful, because other people assume it was luck and tend to be jealous. How do you build the best possible support network for *you*?

3 From the obituary in *The Daily Telegraph*, 9th November 2005.

Building a support network

In her excellent book *Feel the Fear and Do It Anyway*, Susan Jeffers outlines some strategies for surrounding yourself with positive people. She recommends approaching them "to go out and create the kind of support system you want. Even if it seems frightening, do it anyway! It is empowering to have the support of a strong, motivated and inspirational group of people". Her book gives guidance on how to do it, and here is an example of how it worked in practice:

"While doing some consultancy work for the British Dental Association I met the commissioning editor for books, Stephen Hancocks. He suggested we have lunch sometime, and a couple of weeks later rang me to make a date. I was delighted and commented how pleased I was that he had rung to carry this out; he replied that one of his recent New Year's resolutions had been that he was only going to suggest lunch if he meant to do it. We now meet about twice a year and discuss what we are working on and ideas. Our writing areas do not overlap at all: he writes plays and academic articles; I write magazine pieces and books on communications. Yet every time I see him, I come away feeling full of energy and a sense of possibility – and he says he feels the same. It's a case of one plus one equals seven."

The other good strategy for building a support network is to encourage others. What goes around comes around, and if you are the sort of person who writes pleasant emails to others or sends the odd postcard, then hopefully others will be pleased for you and respond in kind. Again, to quote Jeffers:

"You must become what you want to attract. Be the kind of person you would want to surround yourself with."

"I know writers' natural inclination is to be competitive, talk about sales or who's 'good' or 'not good' but it's such a terribly lonely, doubtful life, being around those who understand it should be a good thing. When people send me their work, even if it's terrible shit, I do try to be gentle and constructive, balancing any criticism with some praise. I think it is important to be kind and supportive, and as I've benefited greatly from it, and cannot ever repay those great souls who've helped me on my way, I can only do so for those who come after me, I suppose (though I know how grandiose that sounds from an unpublished writer!)."

Sunil Badami

Other sources of support

"If you want to be a writer, you should do three things: read a lot, write a lot, and be a groupie. Watch arts programmes, profiles and documentaries on writers; listen to *Front Row* on Radio Four as you make your supper and *A Good Read* as you drive to pick up the kids; tune in to *Book Club* on a Sunday afternoon; read *A Life in the Day* of in *The Sunday Times* and listen to *Desert Island Discs*, both of which often feature writers. Read book reviews, even if you can't read all of the books; watch the *South Bank Show* and *Omnibus*, Arena and the Booker Prize TV coverage. I don't think it matters one jot if these writers are people you even read or particularly like, they're all grist for the mill. You might just recognise in them facets of what it is that you are trying to find in yourself."

David Armstrong (see bibliography)

"The best personal support system for a writer is other writing friends. Join an association or club where you will meet like-minded people. It doesn't matter if you're not writing in the same genre; writers are writers. I always recommend *Mslexia* for the nuts and bolts advice, but also for the 'I'm not the only mad woman in the attic' reassurance. When I went to my first RNA[4] writers' weekend, before the mists of time, I was ecstatic to discover that everyone there understood the hours I spent making things up."

Katie Fforde

4 Romantic Novelists Association.

There are professional associations for writers, which help build your sense of yourself as an author. You can join the Society of Authors once you have a contract for a book (not with a vanity publisher) and it is a very good investment. Not only is there a good range of organised meetings, at which interesting people speak, there is an excellent magazine, and they have wonderfully democratic parties at which the famous rub shoulders with the not so famous. The staff are friendly and very supportive; they tend to wander around introducing people to each other and talking to those who look as if they are on their own. But the most useful aspect of membership is a free legal advice service. Submit any contract for their inspection and they will give you a free review, and in my experience publishers tend to give way on points the Society suggests should be queried. Even publishers with very reputable-sounding names, and long charters, try it on with authors, and it is excellent to have the Society of Authors on your side. Most of the meetings are held in London but there are regular get-togethers outside the capital, and a lively branch in Scotland.

There are also some support groups for particular types of fiction. The Romantic Novelists Association is a highly professional association for those who write romantic fiction. The definition of what constitutes romantic is broad, and any form of relationship (between friends, between generations as well as between lovers) counts. The Association runs a valuable New Writers Scheme whereby members can submit a novel, or part of one, for extensive scrutiny feedback by another member. Feedback is anonymous (allowing frankness) but detailed and helpful. Each year the winner of the Association's various awards (best first novel, best romantic novel, best short novel) are widely celebrated. Good parties, a conference and excellent support for a much (and unfairly) derided genre of books.

The Crime Writers Association provides a meeting place for writers in this genre and a sense of camaraderie. The Association organises publications and events, and runs several competitions to award 'Daggers' for excellence in this category of books. In particular, the Debut Dagger, for unpublished crime writers, has been instrumental in launching several promising new authors.

If you decide to publish your own book, you become eligible to join the Independent Publishers Association, which sector the Literary Editor of *The Daily Mail* recently hailed as producing all the most interesting books at the moment.[5] They have an annual conference and run regular meetings. I find the spirit of this organisation really uplifting; there is so much encouragement and positive spirit around.

Many of these organisations have regional branches, which, while heavily dependent on individual members to organise things, can be an excellent source of networking, support and friendship.

Another option is to form your own writing group, either in a specific type of writing (e.g. *Not the Usual Suspects* in detective fiction) or in a specific place; the fastest growing area of these seems to be online writing groups. Many such writing groups spring out of Creative Writing courses. Such groups can be a real motivator for budding writers and provide an incentive deadline for the next lot of material.

> "I have a loose association with two other writers. We all write very different books but we like each other's style and want to read each other's work. We get together a couple of times a year to set practical goals and we then encourage each other, through lack of confidence and simple funk, into sticking to our individual work plan. It works completely because we are different temperaments and don't compete with each other. It wouldn't work for everyone though. We end up being pretty naked to each other. Not everyone is comfortable with that."
>
> Jenny Haddon

Creative Writing courses are a good source of support for budding writers. These vary from undergraduate and postgraduate options, to week-long courses in residential centres. They can make a crucial difference to how you feel about your writing and your ambition to be published.

5 Jane Mays, IPG meeting, December 2004.

"I chewed on another bullet and signed up for a residential writing course. It was expensive and I found it hard to justify, especially to my husband who, although supportive, thought that the outlay for a week away from the children indulging my 'hobby' was a tad excessive – 'if I wanted a break, why didn't I go and stay with my mum?'. I only began to have faith in myself when the tutor pointed out that:

a) if I wanted to go into any other line of business, the outlay for development would probably be thousands, not just a couple of hundred, pounds and

b) that my book was publishable.

It also made me think: most people who want to take up writing assume that all they have to do is buy a ream or two of paper, and that's all the expense they will incur. The fact is, if you are really determined to succeed, you need to put in more than that; there are books to buy, courses to go on, associations to join and so on. Raw talent can't be taught but an awful lot of basic technique can. If you're really sure you want to write a book that you will be proud of, you need to buy in the skills to produce it."

Catherine Jones

On the other hand, as Stephen King pointed out:

"It is, after all, the dab of grit that seeps into the oyster's shell that makes the pearl, not the pearl-making seminars with other oysters."

Contact details for all the above can be found in the Appendix.

Writers are difficult to live with

Overheard at the Edinburgh Book Festival:

"Just because I planned to write all day and cannot, does not mean I want to be reminded of this."

"I don't like it when people bring me coffee when I am in the middle of writing. It destroys my mood, and I then feel guilty if I do not stop and make pleasantries with the person who made it for me – which of course takes me further from the creative process. Now how ungrateful does that sound? But you wouldn't interrupt a welder mid-session or a plumber half-way through an important job, and I do wish people would think about my routine and how it feels to be in the middle of something and not to want to be interrupted."

"My wife comes home from work and I go through the motions of asking how her day went, all the while thinking to myself, 'The fuck I care.'"

The writer's character: the split personality
Dorothea Brande isolates three distinct parts of the writer's character, implying that anyone trying to live with a writer is actually living with three people, not just one. She identifies:

- The sensitive person – able to respond with freshness and originality to new things; someone who sees links between things where other people don't.
- The discriminating adult – workman and critic.
- The person with an 'individual endowment of genius'. "The flashes of insight, the penetrating intuitions, the imagination which combines and transmutes ordinary experience into 'the illusion of a higher reality' – all these necessities of art, or, on a humbler level, all these necessities of any interpretation of life, come from a region beyond those we have been studying and learning to control."

But whereas many writers have felt what she calls 'the miracle of being carried along on a creative current', is this something you can feel at secondhand? Writers do not have a good reputation as living companions:

"The picture of the artist as a monster made up of one part vain child, one part suffering martyr, and one part boulevardier is a legacy to us from the last century and a remarkably embarrassing inheritance. There is an earlier and healthier idea of the artist than that, the idea of the genius as a man more versatile, more sympathetic, more studious than his fellows, more catholic in his tastes, less at the mercy of the ideas of the crowd."

Dorothea Brande

Further reasons why writers are difficult to live with

1   We rely on ourselves; we have no one else to blame if it goes wrong (although we often try).

Writers are denied the comfort blanket on offer to the employees of large organisations, where, when something goes wrong, the response can be 'what are *we* going to do about this?'. Writing is up to *you*. An editor half your age may reject your book on the grounds that it is not right for the market. You may feel you know the market (which consists of people like you) better than she does – but ultimately, if she is offering you the prospect of being published, it is up to you to rewrite until she is happy. No one else can do this for you. (Actually, they can – most publishing contracts specify that if you are unwilling or unable to update your book for future editions, the publisher reserves the right to find someone else to do the work and deduct the costs from your royalties. This feels horrible.)

2   We are subject to the vagaries of fashion.

Ideas for books go in and out of fashion, and the personnel commissioning and managing those ideas move on. Writers may find their ideas unwanted 'leftovers' when personnel change, or themselves stranded by time and no longer of interest.

"You may have written the wrong kind of book at the wrong time, and fashions in publishing are always changing, so what was the wrong book this year might be the right book two or three years down the line."

Margaret James

While it may be true that 'writers create fashion, we follow'[6], in practice you have not only to create the fashion but also persuade others to back you. This is *not* newfangled nonsense:

6 Kate Rowland, Creative Director of New Writing, BBC, talking to the Society of Authors, Spetember 2005.

"Every great and original writer, in proportion as he is great and original, must himself create the taste by which he is to be relished."

William Wordsworth (1770–1850)

3 The creative powers that enable us to do what we do are not infinitely sustainable, and most of us worry about being able to maintain the reputation we have already established.

"What is writing a novel like? The beginning: A ride through a spring wood. The middle: The Gobi desert. The end: Going down the Cresta Run ... I am now (p166 of *The Buccaneers)* in the middle of the Gobi desert."

Edith Wharton (1862–1937), US novelist

"My novel is so terrific that I cannot put pen to paper."

Christopher Isherwood (1904-86)

4 Most of us don't earn much.

Stellar advances are paid to those with agents whose faces fit; most of us just get by. The last income survey of all members of the Society of Authors took place in 2000:

"Three-quarters of the members earned less than the national average wage; two-thirds earned less than half the national average wage; and half earned less than an employee on the national minimum wage."

Kate Pool, *Author Magazine*, Summer 2000

Obviously, this can impede our progress in life as we had planned it – or more significantly, life as those who live with us had planned it. Most of what we do earns nothing until it gets published – and sometimes, not even then.

Actors complain that the general public now know the term 'resting' and will use it with an amused *bonhomie* which suggests that they know you are really not very good. Writers often view suggestions that they should 'consider self-publishing' or make a sudden change of format or genre to produce something more immediately saleable, in the same light.

"Writing is the only profession where no one considers you ridiculous if you earn no money."

Jules Renard (1864–1910), French writer

"I would hesitate to suggest that one can make a living from writing books. Even the best authors struggle, so most of us will have to accept that it is a part-time indulgence."

Edward Denison

5 We can be moody and suspicious.

Other writers' success is infuriating and puts us in a bad mood. We read bad signs into conversations that have taken place, and spot the hidden meaning in emails. Or, as the most recent Chairman of the Society of Authors, Anthony Beevor, told the 2005 AGM:

"Every writer who is honest knows that they are paranoid."

6 We are single-minded.

When a writer is in full flow they are not easily interrupted. We forget about the child we are meant to be bathing and dream about our plot; we day-dream during conversations with other people. This can make us maddening to live with.

"I used to be able to make all my other circumstances subservient to my art. I admit, however, that by so doing I became a bit crazy."

Ludwig van Beethoven (1770–1827)

7 Our work rhythms do not necessarily fit with family life.

It can be difficult to fit writing time with family life. Meal times can be scheduled, but if you are writing well, time and hunger often mean little. Writing is one of the few professions where time really does stand still. This demands accommodation on the part of families:

"When I first married a professional singer, and we almost immediately had a small child, I found it difficult to make our lives fit together. Eating just before practice (let alone performance) was difficult for him, and he liked his food to be practically cold before he would eat it, because hot food could damage his throat and hence his voice – and this of course meant that meals could never be eaten when they were ready. The arrival of our daughter made things problematic – she needed set times to eat. We talked about this and had to develop strategies that would enable us to have family time together, and in fact our daughter's rhythms and his fitted together better than his and mine did, so it was me that had to change. It was not easy, but my body clock has now got used to our compromises, and just as I have heard that for those who miss salt out of their diet, very soon everything tastes too salty, I now find tepid food the only way to eat! It's part of his profession, just as living with a City businessman would involve high expenditure on buying, and maintaining, double-cuffed shirts."

"I find I have to curb my impatience when I have to attend family gatherings and not think too much about how I would much rather be at my desk."

8 We tend to sleep badly.

Good ideas often arrive in the middle of the night, teased out by the workings of our subconscious. The trouble is that other people tend to get woken up when this happens. Then there are plots that won't let us sleep properly, anxiety about deadlines, and just plain insomnia. This is hard to live with.

How to boost the morale of a writer – top tips for those in the supporting role

Don't fire questions at us about progress
This flies in the face of general wisdom, where a specific question is seen to be the true mark of interest. But writers can be so sensitive. A general question on progress goes down better than a deep probe.

Don't keep asking how it is going; if we 'have heard from x or y'. It's a bit like asking a teenager how their exam revision is going – you both know it needs to be done, but don't want to keep being reminded of it. I remember at school, the sure sign that someone was involved in a serious relationship was that they did not want to talk about it, and the same goes for writing. Talking about what you are writing may well stunt your ability to continue; hearing things you plan to write about verbalised may make them sound trite.

The process of getting published is such a rollercoaster that a telephone conversation with an agent or publisher can leave you feeling wildly optimistic. Because you are a creative soul, you can allow your imagination to take flight – which can make the fall to earth even more depressing.

Allow us to reconnect with you slowly

When you emerge from writing hard, your brain is geared into talking through your fingers rather than through your mouth. This is an intense experience and some transition is needed before we can reconnect properly with the rest of the world. If you really want to encourage us, the best advice is to take it slowly and silently. Let us emerge into conversation gradually; just being in the same room may be enough to start with. Head or finger massage, running a bath, a cup of tea, a quick fix of sugar (I like cakes with icing), watching *Neighbours*, all may be excellent ways of allowing us slowly to reconnect with the rest of the world.

When I first had a baby, I used to put him to bed in the evenings and then have a bath, which seemed to symbolise the distinction between his bit of the day and mine. I find the same thing works well with writing – marking the transition from one activity to another gives me something to look forward to, and a point at which I reconnect with everyone else.

And in case this book falls into the hands of a non-writer, I am aware of how 'posey' these two paragraphs sound, thank you.

Don't keep telling us how successful other people are

Hearing at first or second hand about how well someone else is doing is seldom motivating to a writer.

"Nothing grows well in the shade of a big tree."

Constantin Brancusi (1876–1957), refusing fellow
sculptor Rodin's invitation to work in his studio

Do show that you take us seriously

This can be done in many different ways, from talking you up in front of other people to displaying your most recent feedback on the kitchen noticeboard and pointing it out to people to read and be impressed by. Send copies of articles to your parents and friends; talk it up at dinner parties; video/record any publicity highlights. Take pleasure in what is achieved.

If we are trying to write from home, please treat it as a job rather than free time in which to arrange the car insurance, supervise homework and do the shopping. Whereas in truth domestic distractions can be a wonderful way of allowing your mind to play with work in progress, if the day's programme is detailed as a series of jobs it can be hard to take oneself seriously.

Encourage us to take a break

Physical exercise is a good way of improving concentration; sitting at your desk for hours on end is not.

"I am a great believer in the importance of exercise for stimulating the brain, and am greatly enjoying the rowing course I do now and the water sports one I have just started. I definitely feel inspired when I get back to the PC to get writing again."

Jackie Steinitz

Summary

Of course, it is ultimately up to the writer to be clear about what kind of personal support they need, and then to try and resource it. There are no rules about what works best, or even continually – this is highly individual. Some writers work best at times of personal anguish, and both anger and neglect can be effective parents of good writing; others need harmony, quiet, and ministering angels to deliver cookies and hot chocolate on a regular basis. The important thing is to identify the personal circumstances that help you produce your best work.

Questionnaire

So turn now to the questionnaire and decide how good your support mechanisms are. Make a practical assessment right now, but bear in mind how what you have could be improved, so that when, in a few months' time, you come to review your score, you have some contacts to build upon. Mark yourself out of ten.

5

How well-established is your writing habit?

Peter Cook, on running into an old friend: "What are you up to these days?"
Old friend: "I'm writing a book."
Peter Cook: "Neither am I."

We writers can use our time in various ways. We may spend it planning to write, thinking what to write about, tackling the things that must be done before we start to write, meeting with others who encourage us in our desire to write and so on. The options are endless. But, ultimately, only one activity will help us achieve our goal, and that is getting down to doing the writing.

Consideration of your 'writing habit' is vital for any would-be writer; it's the one thing we cannot dodge. All the writers I have spoken to agree on this. If you write a sentence, even if it is a bad sentence, it can always be improved. If you write nothing, but continue to dream of writing the perfect sentence, then your published work is further away than ever. Confucius's famous remark that a 'journey begins with a single step' has never been more relevant.

"In other jobs you can look, even feel, busy when you're not. With writing you can't. You either write or you don't."

Nicholas Allan

"All my life I've been frightened of at the moment I sit down to write."

Gabriel Garcia Marquez (b1928), Colombian novelist

"Blank pages inspire me with terror."

Margaret Atwood[1]

How do other people do it?

Writers have always been fascinated by how others write. Go to any talk by a writer, and for every detailed question about plot or character there will be at least one on the mechanics of writing: pencil or computer; home or office; early mornings or late nights; six years or six months; alcohol or Perrier; flapjacks or bananas. Perhaps our collective hope is that if we understand how the process works for other people, we can imitate their success. Some writers will talk about it; others draw back – perhaps because it feels invasive, like describing how you kiss someone, or through a fear that if you describe something so essential you compromise ever being able to do it again.

Keats apparently could only write if he put on a clean shirt. Others like to write in their pyjamas; they want nothing to get in the way of waking up and starting work (also ensuring, I suppose, that they have to stick at it and can't nip out to the shops). Some have a particular garment to put on, which becomes a talisman for their writing. Others have favourite places: Philip Pullman has a hut at the bottom of the garden; Jacqueline Wilson likes writing on trains. I have always thought that Daphne du Maurier's habit of writing in the morning, followed by long walks with her children in the afternoon, sounded ideal.

"When I'm writing for performance I write best with my 'playwright's trousers' on. This is an incredibly battered old pair of Abercrombie and Fitch scruffs in very heavyweight cotton with umpteen pockets, bits hanging off and compartments which look like they were owned by a long-suffering workman from about the 1950s. It was a pair I bought in New York just before my drama school audition. They are so 'not the usual me' that I knew the moment I tried them on that I had to buy them there and then, and that I'd get offered a

1 Quoted in *The Courage to Write*, Ralph Keyes (see bibliography).

place for sure – and I did! I've done my very best work when wearing them at the keyboard and in the rehearsal room. Completely daft but absolutely true."

Stephen Hancocks

"Rituals are important. I always make coffee in a special cup, and I wear a long quilted dressing gown over my clothes to write. I hate being 'dressed up' to write. I don't want tight bests or an elaborate hairstyle. I want to feel 'free'. Maybe this reflects the freedom one is searching for in being able to go deep into one's psyche – or other people's psyches, when creating characters."

Wendy Perriam

"I like to feel as comfortable as possible, so being in a pair of casual silk trousers, cashmere jumper with a glass of whiskey and no noise is close to my idea of heaven."

Edward Denison

Several people referred to writing as something you train for, building up your stamina to increase your output.

"You will find there is a certain number of words that you can write easily and without strain. When you have found that limit, begin to push it ahead by a few sentences, then by a paragraph or two. A little later try to double it before you stop the morning's work."

Dorothea Brande, writing in the 1930s (and before the advent of the
modern timed gym schedule, of which her advice reminds me)

"I did have to play games with myself to get it done. Like going to the gym – you don't think about the exercise, you just think about getting out of the house with your kit. Likewise, all I had to do was actually get up the stairs and sit down in front of the machine. Afterwards, there wasn't much else to do there but write."

Bernard Lyall

"Decide what times of the day it suits you to write, and for how long. Turn off the phones, disconnect the Internet, and sit there for that time. Words will come. For a first draft, decide how many words it's reasonable to expect yourself to write in that time. If you hit that target early, you can stop (but you probably won't want to). Keep a word count every day, and write it down, so you can pat yourself on the back for those hundred new words, even if nothing else. For later drafts and revisions, make a list of what you want to do and tick it off, for the same sense of achievement."

Emma Darwin

"My book is quite short but took a year to write as my time was so limited. I am old, with a house to run and a severely asthmatic husband to care for. I tried, and usually managed, to snatch two hours in the morning, though not every day, and occasionally I was able to do a bit more in the evening while my spouse dozed in front of the TV. There were times when I nearly gave up."

Bee Kenchington

"Work as a journalist comes in handy; you have to discipline yourself to meet self-imposed deadlines otherwise there's a danger of drift. Regular breaks away from the screen are a must, to have moments when you just forget about writing completely. A walk helps; a visit to the pub is even better. I try to write whenever I have time and train journeys are good."

Adam Powley

"A contract helps, so does a room of one's own, of course. But also – and I got this from Enid Bagnold (subject of my first biography), who got it from HG Wells – never finish at the end of a chapter, or even the end of an idea. Always leave your work in mid-stream so that you don't have to feel like you are starting a new book with every chapter ... and go into your study whether you have anything to write or not; write a letter or diary, make others understand that this is what you do."

Anne Sebba

In his book *On Writing*, Stephen King says he writes for four to six hours every day:

"If I don't write every day, the characters begin to stale off in my mind – they begin to *seem* like characters instead of real people."

He recommends not having phone or Internet available, and shutting the door on the place where you write so that the space becomes fully yours. He also repeats the useful advice offered to him at the very beginning of his career by the editor of a local newspaper: writing with the door closed for the first draft, when you are writing for yourself, and writing with the door open for the second draft, when you are writing for your intended reader. This intended reader may be an actual or imagined person, but must be a real person whose reactions can be targeted.

"There's no question of not feeling like working, I simply sit down and work. Writing comes from the subconscious mind, which is actually quite docile if you tell it what to do. I tell myself to work at such and such a time, and do it. It helps that I have been practising meditation for over 30 years. It has given me more of a 'rapport' to the creative part of my mind. We work together.

Set yourself a definite time for working, and stick to it. Early morning is best, as the mind is uncluttered with thoughts. If you go to bed with the knowledge that you'll be writing first thing in the morning, the mind obeys quite willingly. I get up early, make myself a cup of tea, and sit at the computer at 4.00 a.m. I write till 6.30 a.m. while writing the first draft."

Sharon Maas

"I recommend just forcing yourself to sit there and write something. The most unhelpful displacement activity is deciding that there is another bit of research you must do first."

Professor Gwyneth Pitt

"When I don't feel like writing, I ignore such feelings, knowing that the actual process of writing may well displace them. I would advise would-be authors not to open their post or look at their emails until after their writing stint. It's all too easy to get diverted, distracted or thrown by a worrying letter or email. Keep the phone on 'answer'. Phone calls eat into your writing time. Leave the chores till later. Put your first and best energies into the writing itself. This of course may be impossible if you have children, an outside job, or a sick partner."

Wendy Perriam

"If I'm writing prose and I need to kick-start my brain, I usually read some of my own prose, something I'm pleased with. It's useful to inspire yourself; otherwise; on a bad day, you'll convince yourself that you're rubbish. You're not rubbish.

Making peppermint tea is my displacement activity. Sometimes I'll 'forget' to eat. That's not to be encouraged. You need a screen break anyway, and a healthy lunch gives you energy. (This is basic-seeming advice, but there's no magic wand.) My best inspiration is a deadline. There's no better way of getting your arse in gear. If an article or script or book needs writing by a particular date, write it on a post-it note and have it to hand at all times. Draw a ring round the date on a visible calendar. I remember Eddie Braben, chief writer for Morecambe and Wise, saying he kept his gas bill out to inspire him. Good one."

Andrew Collins

"I never feel like working. The thing to cultivate is habit, not shock therapy. If you write every day whether or not you feel like it, then what you feel like will soon become irrelevant."

Philip Pullman

Where to do the writing

Herein lies the rub. Writing seldom yields an immediate income, so funding a special space in which to work can seem either profligate or simply unaffordable. Most of us must make do with what we have, scribbling as and when we can. Yet having somewhere to do the writing can have a big impact on whether or not anything is achieved.

These days Virginia Woolf's campaign for a 'room of one's own' in which to write is more often negotiated within the context of the allocation of space at home. My first office was in an upstairs bedroom that overlooked the front of our house. In many ways this was perfect: it had a low ceiling which felt cosy, and warmed up quickly if I switched the fan heater on. I could not be seen from the ground floor (which discouraged visitors from ringing the door bell) yet I had a commanding view of the road – so that for the time I occupied this room, I like to think I *was* the Neighbourhood Watch, seeing the comings and goings of all. After two years we moved away and by the time we came back, my children really needed a bedroom each, so I had to find somewhere else. This time I moved into the downstairs 'study' (estate-agent speak for very small room).

Now I was within sight of the front door and liable to be interrupted by people who would say 'I could see you were in so just called by'. I was also distracted by the squabbles over parking, which from above I had been able to view as an interesting socio-logical interaction. The atmosphere was dark and rather drear. We eventually built a loft extension and I now have a room from which I cannot hear the front door bell if I choose not to, have a view over trees and roofs, and am vastly better able to con-centrate. Admittedly it was an expensive solution, but one which I worked towards through book and article sales.

> "I always write in this office at home. I can see birds in the trees outside my window. That's handy. Birds are good for my soul."
>
> Andrew Collins

A local writer friend moved house because her existing property had a bad atmosphere for her. After several years of just feeling that the house was not right, its precise problems were eventually linked to the existence of an underground stream. After finding an alternative property she sent the plans to an expert, who divined it using rods and confirmed that all was well. The downstairs has two reception rooms, one of which is given over to her writing.

If you can't secure a special room to write in, having a space where you can leave your things uninterrupted is important. Somehow the positioning of papers is part of the creative process, and being able to slip back into the same order helps create the mentality to write. Children can be poor respecters of other people's space within the home, so if you find your things being disturbed, try laying a large tablecloth (or an old net curtain) over the space to mark it off as private. It's a good thing for kids to understand that there is some corner of the home that is for their parents only – just as they like you to knock before entering their rooms.

"The working-at-home syndrome has so many downsides: people don't take you seriously, mothers and sisters call you, there are the temptations of checking emails and making yet another coffee. But tell people, with confidence: 'I am a writer.' Don't ever say: 'I just work at home.' Or else rent a studio or go to local library, but never put off the time you start. By 9.00 a.m. I am in my study come what may. I break for lunch at 1.00 p.m. to listen to the news. If you don't answer the phone or screen calls people may think you are precious … But so what? Your work is precious.

The obvious upside of working at home is that you don't waste time travelling or dressing for work. An 80-year-old friend of mine used to say to me, when I bemoaned the fact that all the other mothers at the school gate looked so smart and coiffed and elegant, as if they had spent the whole day preparing for collection duty – and they probably had – 'But you are a writer. That is your badge, wear it with pride.'"

Anne Sebba

"Well, peace and quiet are important, though I have been known to write whole chapters on my laptop with Cbeebies blaring in the background. Beggars can't always be choosers. My most productive times so far have been abroad, on holiday, far away from ordinary life and its distractions. Staying at my sister's place in New York by the sea was wonderful. I would slip down to her big basement for a few hours, while the children ran riot upstairs.

In an ideal world, I think I'd convert the garage at the end of our garden into a study. I could see myself sitting there in years to come, an eccentric old lady, weaving stories. I'd be just far enough away from the family not to be distracted, but near enough to feel close, still. They could bring me cups of tea and homemade chocolate cake every now and again. Bliss!"

Emma Burstall

I like writing in bed with my laptop on my knees. It's very comforting as the machine warms up, it's like holding a hot water bottle. A comfortable chair is particularly important, as is good light, whether artificial or natural. I like to be able to open the window quickly and dislike the hum of air conditioning in modern offices. Pay attention to what puts you in a good mood for writing.

You should also collect around you things that support your writing. I have heard Philip Pullman explain the importance of elastic bands to ping and paperclips to unfold as part of the process of getting ready to write. Other people read the newspapers, or a particularly loved author. I have lots of pictures in my writing room, and have a copy of Vermeer's *Girl with a Pearl Earring* positioned so that if I look up above my computer screen she is looking back at me. I always treat myself to a gorgeous calendar.

> "On some days I might take my laptop to another room, as my study-bedroom seems cramped at times and the window is small and has to have the blind down on sunny days. Downstairs is still high up and has bigger, north-facing windows, which don't need to be shaded. In the early mornings it is nice to feel cosy, but later in the day I feel I need some space."
>
> Sheila Cornelius

When to write

Time is always short, but no life is that busy that you can't carve out some time for what you really want to do. Dorothea Brande saw planning your writing time as vital, and she suggested looking through your diary, making a time when you are going to write, and then to sticking to it. ("You have given yourself your word and there is no retracting it.") Then try promising to write at different times of the day. ("You must learn to disregard every loophole the wily unconscious points out to you. If you fail repeatedly at this exercise, give up writing. Your resistance is actually greater than your desire to write, and you may as well find some other outlet for your energy early as late.")

In *The Seven Habits of Highly Effective People* (see bibliography), Stephen R Covey discusses how we spend our time, and whether or not it is being allocated according to what we want to achieve, rather than to other (or other people's) priorities. Are you concentrating on the non-important urgent things on your 'to do' list which give a quick buzz in that they allow you to tick things off and feel busy, or the important non-urgent, which means you are thinking in good time about the 'main effort' – things that are really important to you. This is an excellent thing for writers to dwell upon.

> "So often I sit down at my desk when I get to work and think, I'll just deal with my emails then get onto that major piece of work. Then the emails expand, and no time is left to do what I had planned to do. The thing to do is to tackle what you want to do first, and then fit all the other things around it. That way you leave the office feeling satisfied rather than that you have wasted your time and done nothing significant all day."
>
> Arts Administrator

Having noticed that several writers of my acquaintance inscribe 'writing' in their diaries or put a line through time when they know they cannot be interrupted, I have started to do the same. It helps me prioritise, and emphasise to myself that writing is really important.

If there are other people in the house while you are writing, be clear with yourself about the practical circumstances under which you will come out of your writing space (dire emergency only, or lost socks?), and how long you will take a break for without implying that you have given up for the day. Along similar lines, can you draw a link between the circumstances of your life and a good mood for writing? For example, how do the following affect your writing abilities the next day – wine, spirits, eating late, eating early, relaxing before you go to bed, particular types of music? Dwelling on such things is not neurosis; it is part of your working method, in the same way that footballers learn to like particular sports drinks or clothing, or teachers to rely on specific textbooks. A golfer on *Desert Island Disks* recently said he had hundreds of copies of the soundtrack from *The Lion King* because he liked a particular track to be the last thing he heard before getting out of the courtesy car to play, so carried a copy for every potential driver. Getting others to respect your commitment to writing is easier if you show that you take it seriously yourself. People tend to take you at your own estimation.

> "Writing time is your time; you need to claim it for yourself, often against the demands of other people. Sometimes this may feel like a military strategy and it is quite in order to treat it in this way: to plot and plan to take the fortress which is your imaginary castle, your silent, fertile abode, despite the background of your everyday tasks and obligations. When you begin to feel guilty, remind yourself that it's for the child's sake."
>
> Julia Casterton (see bibliography)

> "I am at my best early in the morning, but if the novel is going well I can work from six one morning to two the next and then get up and do the same again. You get beyond tired because you are in a different world and just want to climb back into it again. When it is finally finished and you have to emerge, it's hard to know what to do with yourself."
>
> Trisha Ashley

> "I generally only write in the mornings, or up to about 2.00 p.m., with some very short breaks. I have been known to go on much longer, but I always regret it because I feel physically stagnant and strained and it is difficult to relax afterwards. I listen to Radio 3 or some cengle CD music, like Mozart, or Satie, played very low so that I am hardly aware of it. I think it makes me feel less lonely and isolated. I can work in silence at the library, but then I feel the comfort of others' presence and there is always some kind of movement going on so there is no sense of isolation."
>
> Sheila Cornelius

> "I'm a morning person. I'm writing this before breakfast. You can't turn yourself into a morning person, but if you are, like me, you'll wake up thinking about what you're writing. I can't wait to get my

computer on in the morning and wish I didn't have to shave! (I always do shave, and that's a tip in itself: there's a temptation when you're writing to be a slob – but if you shave and shower and get dressed, you'll feel a whole lot better about yourself.) Let the writing rule your life to an extent, but keep it in perspective. Never put yourself in a position where you're opening the door to the postman in your dressing gown! I can start as early as 7.00 a.m., but I never write after 7.00 p.m. *Channel Four News* – I must watch it, so I must finish by that time. The evenings are family time."

Andrew Collins

"I try and write in the mornings, but I always end up sitting with a whiskey in the evening and writing until past midnight, which makes it harder to write the next morning. And so it continues! I think one has to try and liberate one's self from external constraints. Without sounding trite, one needs to free the mind. If you believe in something enough, it is easy to maintain momentum."

Edward Denison

"I have to do most of my writing in the evenings once the children are in bed. It's hard, when I get in from work and just want to relax and watch mindless TV or read the paper. But I think having a deadline really helps. You tell yourself you won't be working this hard forever, there's an end to it – until the next book, of course. And the reward – seeing yourself in print – will make it all worthwhile."

Emma Burstall

"I'm a terrible procrastinator and will find a million things to do to avoid having to sit down – it's funny how urgently the lintels will need dusting or I have to find out about Surinam at nine o'clock – but eventually I will settle down around ten o'clock and work through. Once I've started, I do tend to keep working, though I will take regular breaks – walking around the room, smoking, etc."

Sunil Badami

The bottom line is that if the writing is important to you, you will find some time to do it:

"... the writer is someone who acquires the capacity for organising and constructing daily life in order to be capable of writing effectively, with a real sense of growth and development."

Malcolm Bradbury (see bibliography)

Avoiding other commitments

Another thing to consider is how distractable you are from writing. Which additional activities help your writing effort, and which get in the way? Author Beryl Bainbridge has paid tribute to the low advances paid by publishers, which forced her to fill her time with interesting paid activities, which in turn gave her more to write about. But there is a danger that you take on so many extra-curricular activities that you feel frustrated by your lack of time to write.

In general, low-level and routine activities can stimulate creativity – I find hanging the washing out always gives me a fresh take on my writing. Activities that require a higher level of 'mind involvement' can leave me feeling stimulated if they are short, but utterly drained if they take all day. For the last couple of years I have been teaching an MA class at Kingston University on Thursday mornings, and the hour-and-a-half-long session, first thing in the morning, usually sets me up for a really good day's writing – because I have got my brain going and practised being articulate. But a whole day in the classroom, or long meetings in stuffy rooms, can leave me feeling I have nothing left to give, either verbally or on the page.

Learning to say no is a very skilled art, and one that takes practice. In general, thanking the person needing help for asking you, but saying 'I don't feel able to commit to that right now' is a good way out, as it implies that the 'no' is not for ever. Susan Jeffers advises that if you do say no to things, you should 'have a bigger yes burning inside' so you use the time you saved for your main goal.

What will you write with?

Some writers prefer to write by hand; others using a computer.

Advantages of writing by hand

- You can refine and shape your sentences as you write them. Because the physical effort of writing is hard, you may think more carefully about trying to come up with the right word in the first place rather than seeing all your writing as refinable later (as happens when you use a computer – nothing is ever final).

- It's easier to see what your first thought was because you can still see the correction. There are computer programs that do this for you, but I find being methodical with a computer is the opposite of letting your ideas flow freely.

"Between my finger and my thumb
The squat pen rests; snug as a gun …
I'll dig with it."

Seamus Heaney (b1939), Irish Poet, from *Digging, Death of a Naturalist*

"I believe that writing on paper makes me write better. It's too easy on the word processor to put it all in, or to use an approximate word instead of the absolutely right one, thinking 'Oh, I can change it later.' But you never do, because the very fact that the words are filtered through a screen gives them a spurious authority. Whereas doing it on paper means that the sheer time it takes to transmit the thought to the hand (I write beautifully clearly, but infuriatingly slowly, a huge problem in exams) gives me time to find the right word or phrase rather than the approximate one, making my language more precise."

Cathy Douglas

"I write a little bit every day. I enjoy using beautiful notebooks and writing by hand."

Jacqueline Wilson

"I use a Mont Blanc fountain pen, not because I'm a snob (particularly), but because it's the only pen I've found which flows. It's also the pen traditionally used by people who sign treaties, so it makes me feel I'm writing something important. Machiavelli used to write in his finest clothes for the same reason."

Nicholas Allan

"I write by hand in red exercise books, as I did as a child."

Wendy Perriam

"Although my pieces are written up and further constructed on a word processor, the initial 'layering of the landscape' is achieved with a sharp HB pencil, a wad of new paper and a clean white eraser. This method of creation, I think, is pure, free from electronic distraction and infinitely and immediately alterable."

Molly Cutpurse

"Writing wills used to be a simple business. You thought about the circumstances, the possible eventualities and drafted one to match. The advent of the computer meant they suddenly got longer, because all the material you had drafted for others 'just in case' could be put into every will you wrote. The result is that the standard will has extended in length dramatically and is no longer as personally written for the individual."

Solicitor

Writing a book by hand is a physical process, for which some writers prepare very carefully:

"I do not start writing until I have a clear outline in my head of what the book is for, what I want to say and how I will develop my argument. I then prepare for writing in a ritualistic way. I buy a new pen and a fancy new notebook – it has to be one with squared paper in it; these are difficult to find in the UK, although standard on the continent, and I usually get mine from Paperchase on the concourse of Euston station. I clear a physical space for the writing, which I like to be uninterrupted while the process is going on. At the moment I am using the dining table because both my own study, and that of my late wife, are full to bursting with paperwork. While I am writing I do not like to be interrupted, so although I will answer the phone, I always arrange to talk later. I do not have a computer at home; this was a deliberate decision after leaving academia. I found that emails ate into my time, and I could end up achieving nothing more during the day than answering – or feeling guilty about not answering – queries from other people. I decided to put my energy into writing down what I do think rather than correcting other people's erroneous versions of my ideas.

My writing process is very straightforward. Firstly I write an outline of the entire book, and then I break this down into chapters and expand the argument already outlined in full. I write long hand and find that by doing this I think about the words I use more carefully than if I were to type. The book is then passed to my former departmental secretary Jenny, who types it up for me. She hands it back, and after a read-through and an edit it is ready for the publisher. I have used this writing process for many years now, and am convinced that thinking carefully about what I want to say, before I say it, leads to clearer communication. The first book in the series (of four so far) has been reprinted 19 times since it was published in 1981, so this method of writing seems to work for me."

Peter Checkland, Emeritus Professor of Systems, Lancaster University

Advantages of the computer

- It's easier to produce stream-of-consciousness writing as the words flow straight through your fingers onto the keyboard. You really can write almost as fast as you think.

- You can be more objective about your own work. If you have a tendency to get distracted by your own handwriting, seeing it typed in front of you allows you to be more critical.

- It's less physically tiring for your fingers (but far more tiring on the eyes, so be sure to look up at regular intervals from the screen and into the distance, to stretch the muscles that hold your eyes in place – otherwise, it can ruin your eyesight).

- You can read what you wrote. Like many writers I keep a pad of paper and a pen next to my bed, but I often can't read what I wrote in the middle of the night! (There are people who use dictaphones in the wee small hours, to capture their thoughts, and there is software that can download this straight onto the screen, but if you share a bed this has always seemed rather anti-social to me.)

"I love my laptop! It's an old IBM and it's only become an object of affection as it's become older and slower. I used to have an old Macintosh laptop, which I loved because I'd written so much on it – it had ten years of my work on its hard drive, and I thought of it as a friend. I suppose knowing where all the keys are, and the feeling of the 'right' kind of pressure are important; I like the way that some of the keys have run smooth, and there's crumbs between them. I suppose if I got a new computer, it might be faster or have more storage or a bigger screen, but it would take a while for me to develop the same intimacy I have with the one I've got now.

I always keep small Moleskin notebooks on me – the tiny ones that come three to a pack. They're small enough to put in a pocket or a bag, and I jot down story ideas or stick clippings from odd pages of the newspaper in them. I think they're great – they feel 'writerly' and they're very sturdy. I have one that's been around the world with me for three years – I do consult it for ideas and am always interested when I re-read it – though perhaps it's like a dream journal, interesting to the owner but overwhelmingly boring for everyone else."

Sunil Badami

Your writing method

"Write as rapidly as possible, with as little attention to your own processes as you can give. Try to work lightly and quickly, beginning and ending each sentence with a good, clear stroke. Re-read very little – only a sentence or two now and then to be sure that you are on the true course … At the time of writing, nothing is more confusing than to have the alert, critical, over-scrupulous rational faculty at the forefront of your mind."

Dorothea Brande

"I worked as a publisher and editor before writing full time, and I found one of the hardest things to do was to switch off my critical faculty while I was writing. The solution I came up with was to write on a word processor, but to make the text on screen so small that I cannot read it while I am writing. That way, I cannot correct as I go. I dump onto the screen and then read and edit later."

Elizabeth Edmondson

Write in several stages; the process of writing is rewriting, and few of us get it right first time. One rather alarming tendency in publishing today is the desire of publishers to get authors to produce words that are ready for the printer, eliminating the time (and cost) of editing, and it's not unusual for academic authors to be offered an inducement for delivering a pre-edited manuscript (i.e. no further editing will take place). A couple of years ago I wrote a book for a reference publisher. They provided me with a software template onto which I had to deposit my words. I found it quite impossible to work this way. My brain would release the sentences but what they were asking me to do was edit them onto the page they had prepared to hold them. I found that it required two processes: first the writing (and refining), and then the editing onto the template – a neat way of them avoiding costs. The whole thing took me vastly longer than I had anticipated.

Writing with others

Writing with someone else can be difficult. Approaching the same subject, two writers will probably hit on equally valid solutions, which are nevertheless irreconcilable. But the process can work; it all depends upon personality and circumstances. Best-selling crime writer Nicci French is in fact a husband-and-wife team which operates from different rooms of the house. They comment positively on each other's work and take the story further independently.

Some find there is greater focus and objectivity in working partnerships:

"Working as a co-author was a big advantage for me. I could trust my colleague to tell me what was working and what wasn't, and vice versa."

Adam Powley

And others evolve more unusual writing arrangements:

"My co-playwright (Declan Hill) and I found that with both of us having busy lives, the times we could sit down together were very limited. So we hit on the idea of writing by email. Basically it works rather like the game of consequences. We each start a 'play'. I write page 1 of 'mine' and he writes page 1 of 'his'. One week later we swap by email. Then we each write page 2 of each others', send them back and so on and so forth. At a predetermined time we meet and discuss the development of both pieces and decide how to progress from there. Our very first collaboration using this method gained us a commission, and the play that we then developed using the same technique enjoyed a successful three-week run at the Etcetera Theatre in London. We still work using the same method but with some refinements on agreed plot lines and directions."

Stephen Hancocks

Choosing the right typeface

The typeface you choose on a computer screen can have a big impact on how you feel about your work. I find that I choose fonts to match the audience I am approaching. For several years, and after the font had been found by my children, I used **Comic Sans** – but then seemingly overnight everyone started using it, and I had to change. Now if I see things written in this typeface, my dislike of it gets in the way of reading the text. For more formal documents I use **Times New Roman**, for clarity I use Arial. Getting the font right for a particular work is a bit like having the right music on in the background when you are reading – it becomes a key part of the product.

"When it comes to the choice of fonts on the computer, I seldom stray from **Times New Roman**, set as my default typeface, though not even by me … It is of course a version of a classic typeface, designed for the *Times* newspaper in London in the 1930s, but based on the designs of the great Renaissance typographer Nicholas Jensen, and thus a reminder of the key turning point in the history of Western typography, when the **Gothic Black Letter** styles favoured by Gutenberg and Caxton gave way to the clarity of Roman designs. **Times New Roman** is certainly clear and elegant, but it is also rather sober and old-fashioned. I'm beginning to wonder if it may be affecting my style.

The only other fonts I use with any regularity are **Arial**, set as the default for my Outlook Express e-mail, and `Courier`. **Arial** is as clear as **Times New Roman** and less old-fashioned, but for me it lacks character and beauty. It has a sort of disembodied blandness that maybe suits the medium of email – but I can't imagine composing a poem in **Arial**. `Courier` is rather different: it has a distinctively rough, but attractive typewriter-ish feel, and I use it for pieces of writing where urgency takes precedence over polish."

Harry Eyres, Slow Lane, *Weekend Financial Times*,
27–28th August 2005

Summary

This chapter has detailed a whole lot of considerations, which you may think of as whimsical. Rest assured that they are not. The most important thing for any writer is to find the combination of circumstances that best suits them, and which provides the best environment for writing in. Without doing the writing, you will never get published.

Questionnaire

Now turn to the questionnaire and think about how seriously you take your writing habit. How willingly do you get to your desk? Do you see yourself as a writer whose need to be taken seriously is important, or do you put yourself down and dismiss your desire to write? Do you keep dates with yourself, so that when you have promised yourself you will write you do so, or do you find endless excuses to put off the actual writing? Bearing in mind that if you decide you do really want to write, you can review your commitment later on, give yourself a mark out of ten right now for the effectiveness of your writing habit.

6

Do you have something to write about that others would want to read?

> "There is no more beautiful mission than to create the free novel, than to fabricate a world that we will never reach, regardless of how long we live."
>
> Ramon Gomez de la Serna (1888–1963), Spanish novelist

There are many would-be writers who find that not having a subject immediately to hand stops them getting started. Some are overwhelmed with choice; faced with so many possibilities, how do you decide where to concentrate your efforts? Others are just overwhelmed and don't have an idea at all. It's the *process* of writing they long to be involved in, and the end-result they long to see – but the means of getting there (a subject that will motivate them sufficiently to allow them to keep writing, and do the same for the reader) gets less consideration.

This was a conversation between a newly published writer and a friend's mother-in-law:

Mother-in-law: "I mean to write a book one day."
Writer: "Oh really? Why?"
Mother-in-law: "I have a computer."

"I long to write, and right now I have the time to do so, but I can't find anything to write about. Having struggled with this for ages I eventually came to the conclusion that, as I am only 30, and have so far had a fairly restricted life – I went to university, got married and had two children, and have since then followed my husband around on diplomatic postings – not enough has happened to me to give me material to write about. Rather than carrying on feeling frustrated by not being able to think of a subject, I decided I would wait another five years and see if more had occurred by then to give me something to write about."

"I have decided to write a Mills & Boon novel. I have booked myself on a weekend course and once the children are back at school, I will begin."

My hunch is that these people never will get started. Becoming a writer means not so much looking for things to write about, as being impelled to put into words even the most ordinary of experiences. If you really want to write, not having a subject will not put you off, because you will write about that. The former editor of *The Author* magazine (official publication of the Society of Authors) once told me that the most commonly submitted piece for possible publication was on how it feels to finally get something published. He got two or three of these a week.

"There are significant moments in everyone's day that can make literature. You have to be alert to them and pay attention to them."
Raymond Carver (1838–88), US poet, short story writer and essayist

"I haven't said much about the subject matter of writing. That's because I don't think it matters what the subject is, as long as the writing is alive. A small-scale, unassuming subject is just as worthy of fiction as a sweeping saga with profound philosophical under-pinnings. Fiction is about what it's like to be human, so it can cover the entire range of our experiences.

Some writers know from the start what their subject is and have something they passionately want to say. Other writers discover their subject as they go along. If you have a feeling, no matter how vague, that you'd like to write something, that's enough to start with. As you write, you'll gradually discover what that feeling is about, and what your subject is."
Kate Grenville (see bibliography)

"The more I read, and write, the more convinced I am that good writing has less to do with acquired technique than with inner conviction. The assurance that you have something to say that the world needs to hear counts for more than literary skill. Those writers who hold their readers' attention are the ones who grab them by the lapel and say, 'You've got to listen to what I'm about to tell you.'"

Ralph Keyes (see bibliography)

"To study life you don't have to go on creative junkets and waste public funds. Study life where you live, it's more productive, and cheaper, too."

Vladimir Voinovich (b1932), Russian novelist

'Write about what you know'

"The seaman tells stories of the winds, the plowman of bulls, the soldier details his wounds, the shepherd his sheep."

Sextus Propertius (50?–15?BC), Roman poet

This is the advice most commonly given to would-be writers. However, if you want to be published, you not only need to find something to write about, *you need to find a subject that other people want to read about.*

Books come in many shapes and formats, but a quick study of the stock in any bookshop will show you that these break down into fairly distinctive – and standard – genres.[1] For example, if you want to write a novel, it could be of several sorts. Publishers tend to classify novels according to the kind of read they make; although these are not fixed in stone, and new types do emerge[2], your proposal stands a better chance of being accepted if those

---

1 Or types. In an industry that is packed with new products (the UK alone produces 130,000 new books and new editions each year), if books are packaged into easily identifiable types, it makes it easier for the customer to spot the kind of book they like – and the bookseller to put them where they can be found.

2 For example the emergence of 'crossover fiction' in the last ten years; fiction that can be read by adults and children with equal pleasure, such as Philip Pullman's books.

you are submitting it to can get a clear picture of what it resembles. For example, if you have in your mind a story of one woman's rise from humble beginnings to independence, you could develop it along the lines of the following existing categories:

- 'Clogs and cobbles' (the title comes from the cover illustration; usually a northern tale of gritty determination based on a rise from obscurity to prosperity, e.g. Catherine Cookson)
- 'Sex and shopping' (a novel full of brand names, e.g. Jackie Collins)
- 'Bedroom and boardroom' (e.g. Louise Bagshawe)
- Historical romance (e.g. Philippa Gregory)
- Pure romance (e.g. Mills & Boon)
- Literary fiction (e.g. Joanne Harris)

Non-fiction offers an equally wide range of options. You could probably think of several possible writing projects based on your own life:

- A book on the kind of food you like (how to cook it and what to eat it with)
- A lifestyle book based on a period of your life (how I felt as a child/student/employee)
- An account of a troubling time (overcoming illness, death, divorce)
- A travel memoir
- A historical research project on your family

It is the marrying-up of determination to write and a subject that other people want to read about, that is likely to produce the published writer.

But which matters more, the determination to get into print or finding the right subject? Many years ago I went on a course for those about to start running small businesses. A similar question was asked: What matters more, finding the right business or having the determination to make it work? The tutors were emphatic: the determination to make something work matters far more than the specific opportunity chosen. I think the same works in publishing. If you are really determined to get there, you will. The choice of the right subject will be part of your determination to succeed.

Writing about things you care about

More important than writing about what you know, is writing about what you care about. Writing is seldom an '*à la carte*' choice; it's very difficult to just pick an interesting subject and proceed to develop it into a full-length novel that others would want to read. Publishing would be a risk-free business if this were the case. Rather, most novels seem to begin with a character or a situation that intrigues, and then the writer's ponderings on how that might develop, or affect different characters, may turn the initial thought into a story. Rose Tremain has explained how the origin of *Music and Silence* was a chance remark in a car while on holiday in Denmark. The remark referred to a king's keeping an orchestra beneath his state-rooms so that the music wafted upwards but the musicians were obscured from view. She wondered what it felt like to be part of the invisible orchestra. Her advice to would-be writers was to 'pay attention' to potential ideas that may be passing.

> "If you see me walking along with a glazed expression, it's probably because an idea has just hit me. Ideas are triggered by anything – thoughts, things I see, things someone tells me – and whereas a non-writer would just think, 'How interesting!' I would think, 'How interesting and what a great story that might make!'. But, I never, never, never write the idea down. That would kill it stone dead. Notebooks are for shopping lists, as far as I'm concerned. The idea has to churn around in my head until it gels into characters and becomes much more than just the original idea – which can take days or months or even years (though there will be other ideas churning around too, and I will be writing something else while another idea is growing).

I have a terrible memory but if the idea's good enough it will root itself deeper into my mind and will never be forgotten. It grows by itself, or else it dies – and I never weep for an idea that dies. I have no conscious control over the process, except to give the idea space to grow by itself. When the characters start to speak, I know it's going to work. When the first paragraph comes to me, I start writing. I never plan at all, but the time I spend allowing the idea to grow is essential. How do I know if I've hit a blind alley? That would only happen very early on in the thinking process, well before I started writing – that would just be one of those dead ideas that I don't weep for."

Nicola Morgan

"I have a box on my desk – a Tiffany box, as it happens, which once held a candlestick and which I couldn't bear to throw out – and when I have an idea, or read a news story, or hear an evocative snatch of conversation, I scribble it down on whatever comes to hand, usually in less than 20 words, and chuck it in. Then I forget about it.

When I'm contemplating my next book, usually about half-way through the one I'm currently writing, I dump the contents on my desk and sort through them. Quite often, it's like the recipe you scribble down in the back of your cheque book from a magazine in the hairdresser's: you look at it later and wonder why on earth you imagined it was any use. But there are usually one or two you can try on for size. I take one and roll it round in my mind to see if other ideas will collect and stick to it, a bit like a dung beetle's egg ball collecting sticks and stones and strange shiny things.

At last, with the plot which I will have lived with now for months, or even years sometimes, sufficiently established for me to know where it begins and where I guess it will finish, I'm ready to start. But to avoid the terror of the blank sheet, I always have the first paragraph written in my head and the first characters waiting in the wings to come on stage. Then they take over, and I wait with some fascination to discover what they're going to do."

Aline Templeton

"I don't think the process of deciding what to write about ever really starts – because I never stop thinking about possible stories. I have done it since a child. When I do stop, I'll be dead.

I'm in the habit of generating far more ideas than I can use, but it isn't a particularly formal process. I read masses of non-fiction and things strike me; if they interest me I think about them, chuck them around in my mind for a particularly when I am just falling asleep or waking up. The other day I read an obituary (always read obits) of a woman who was a big-name criminal defence lawyer in the late 1940s and I thought: wow! But I didn't do anything with it except file it away for future reference. But the idea is there now – an historical precedent for what might become a crime series, if I ever manage to write a crime novel ...

What I am doing is trying to find the angle, which might interest me – and therefore a reader. I suppose what I am looking for is some sort of emotional resonance; a big theme underlying the life or the facts that have caught my attention. Then if I find that, I might do a bit more reading on the subject, or surf the web for interesting leads to add to the material. I might make a few notes, but I don't have a sacred notebook. Although I probably should start because my memory isn't quite what it was.

Then if it seems worth pursuing, if I get a rush of ideas and the characters seem to come to life, I will try putting together a story. I try to take it slowly, the danger is of getting ahead of myself; imagining the most fantastic scenes without anything to fit them. I have to say a pet hate of mine is people giving me ideas for stories. This is probably stupid because it ought to be a good source, but they never put it the right way."

Harriet Smart

"I started writing *Where Did It All Go Right?*, my childhood memoir, for myself, with no publisher. I wrote four chapters, convinced it was a good idea (childhood in which nothing traumatic happens, written with self-effacing humour and working in actual childhood diaries which I had kept). I showed it to my agent. She liked it. She sent it to one publisher who ignored it. Then a new editor at Ebury, who had also been charged with finding new authors, approached my agent and asked if certain among her clients had any interest in writing a book. She showed him my sample chapters and a deal was struck. Suddenly, what had begun as a project to please myself was a book. I'll be honest, this book just flowed out of me. The structure was self-governing and I had all my diaries, so it was just a case of getting it down and taking my Ebury editor's advice on tidying it up."

Andrew Collins

"If you can discover what you are like, if you can discover what you truly believe about most of the major matters in life, you will be able to write a story which is honest and original and unique. But those are very large 'ifs', and it takes hard digging to get at the roots of one's own convictions.

If you are unwilling to write from the honest, though perhaps far from final, point of view that represents your present state, you may come to your deathbed with your contribution to the world still unmade, and just as far from final conviction about the universe as you were at the age of twenty."

Dorothea Brande (see bibliography)

Finding out what you think about things

Here is an exercise devised to help the parents of teenagers examine how they feel about moral issues. It may help you establish your own moral viewpoint. Tick the box that most closely reflects your own views on the following extreme positions:

Sex only after marriage	☐☐☐☐☐	Sex before marriage
No adultery	☐☐☐☐☐	Open marriage
Only heterosexual relationships	☐☐☐☐☐	All relationships and lifestyles equally valid
Only natural birth control	☐☐☐☐☐	Contraception freely available
No sex education for children	☐☐☐☐☐	Sex education for all
No abortion	☐☐☐☐☐	Abortion on demand
Chastity for women more important than for men	☐☐☐☐☐	Chastity for men more important than for women
Necessary to have legal age of consent	☐☐☐☐☐	Young people free to make their minds up

| Marriage is forever | ☐☐☐☐☐ | Divorce is always an option |
| Tight controls over sexual scenes on TV[3] | ☐☐☐☐☐ | Media freedom |

"If you find that you are baulking at definite answers to great questions, then you are not yet ready to write fiction which involves major issues. You must find subjects on which you are capable of making up your mind, to serve as the groundwork of your writing. The best books emerge from the strongest convictions – and for confirmation see any bookshelf."

Dorothea Brande

What inspires you?

The notion of 'time famine' is much quoted these days, but as life gets busier, the danger is that you end up on a hamster wheel of commitments, unable to step off. Writers need to be able to harvest thoughts and feelings aside from this, in order to connect with the world.

A couple of years ago I wrote a book on the artist Joseph Cornell.[4] His art-form was arranging items in frames and boxes; displaying them as a harmonious and intriguing whole. As the book I was writing was for children, I offered to work with my son's primary school class. I gave them a talk on Cornell, about when and where he lived – just outside New York. He was active from the 1930s onwards, just as the city skyline began to change with all the skyscraper building. I described some of the things he liked and collected – ballet and cinema programmes, bus tickets, astronomical charts, oval and round-shaped things – and I then asked the children to do the same. We all made lists of what we liked, the teachers and me included. The children did not have to read out their lists (this was private information), but we used this as the basis of collecting for the boxes that they then put together. This turned out to be a remarkably fertile exercise, making us all feel creative.

3 From *Whatever! A Down-to-earth Guide to Parenting Teenagers* by Gill Hines and Alison Baverstock, Piatkus, 2005.
4 *Secrets in a Box*, Prestel Publishing, 2003

Quick exercise

Make a list of 'things' that you like. Here are a few of mine to get you started:

- The smell of new-mown grass
- The opening mechanism for anchovy tins
- The colour yellow – a buttery more than a lemon version
- Furniture made out of walnut wood
- The 1960s television series, *Bewitched*

Some people find out either what they like, or what they think, through writing:

> "Writing alerts you to what you are really interested in."
>
> Paul Magrs, *The Creative Writing Course-book* (see bibliography)

> "I have to write to start to have ideas."
>
> Francoise Sagan[5]

Others find that issues they have explored through their writing seek them out, and it is interesting to speculate whether this is coincidence or subconscious choice. Television producer Harry Thompson wrote about reactions to random cruelty (both characters' wives died of incurable diseases) and then once the book was finished (*This Thing of Darkness*) found he was suffering from inoperable lung cancer. He noted the "football-stadium-sized irony; that the vicious unfair lottery I wrote about should have arrived on my doorstep".

It's also possible that things you know about, while taken for granted by you, fascinate other people. Katy Hickman's *Daughters of Britannia* presented an intriguing portrait of the life of the diplomatic wife. Herself the daughter of a diplomat, she provided access to a world most people know nothing about. So be aware if there is a private world that you could share:

---

5 Quoted in *The Creative Writing Course-book* (see bibliography).

> "I cannot write as well as some people; my talent is in coming up with good stories about lawyers. That is what I am good at."
>
> John Grisham (b1955), novelist

Stephen King's advice is to remain conscious of themes that you are interested in:

> "I was built with a love of the night and the unquiet coffin."

Are your ideas sustainable for a full-length book?

> "Far too many relied on the classic formula of a beginning, a muddle, and an end."
>
> Philip Larkin (1922–85), poet, referring to modern novels

> "The last thing one knows in constructing a work is what to put first."
>
> Blaise Pascal (1623–62), French philosopher

This book is not a writing manual. It is not therefore concerned with taking the would-be writer on a systematic tour from first scribblings through longer pieces to possible publication. There is (of course) a world of difference between beginning to write and spinning a tale into a full-length novel that other people want to read; the process of sustaining an idea or theme for the whole of a novel is much harder than people think. Good ideas can run out of steam; characters become boring; situations seem unresolvable.

> "I had a brilliant (I thought) idea for a novel about army wives. I knew no one else had written one and I was sure there was a market. I decided to bite the bullet and try again. Half-way through the book I discovered I didn't know how to get the characters out of the situation into which I had dumped them, the ending looked extremely dodgy and the story (my brilliant idea) was looking singularly tarnished. In short, I just didn't know how to write a whole book."
>
> Catherine Jones

"The artistic impulse seems not to wish to produce finished work. It certainly deserts us halfway, after the idea is born; and if we go on, art is labor."

Clarence Shepard Day (1874–1935), US writer

A common starting point is to write a series of short stories about related characters, which can become a book. Booker prize winner Pat Barker's first novel *Union Street* works like this, offering a series of individual but connected portraits of the residents.

Others decide to write a book in a style or format that has already been successful. Publishers and agents may say they are always looking for something new, but producing look-alikes of what other publishers have already produced also seems quite common too. It's up to you, but it would be a pity to forsake your own original vision for a pastiche:

"Be true to your own voice, rather than trying to be another Helen Fielding or Nick Hornby or whoever. Don't worry about 'what will sell', but express the world in the unique individual way that you see it and experience it."

Wendy Perriam

"Better to write for yourself and have no public, than to write for the public and have no self."

Cyril Connolly (1902–74), British writer and journalist

So, as you conduct your search for a subject that you care about and others will want to read about, remember:

"There are only two essential rules: one, that the novelist should deal only with what is within his reach, literally or figuratively (in most cases the two are synonymous), and the other that the value of a subject depends almost wholly on what the author sees in it, and how deeply he is able to see into it."

Mrs Wharton, *The Confessions of a Novelist* (*Atlantic Monthly*, quoted in Dorothea Brande, written in 1934)

How do you decide when you have hit a blind alley?

"I spent about two years on and off working on a crime novel inspired by the James Bulger murder case. The idea I still think is sound – what if a child was wrongly imprisoned for murdering another child? – but I didn't have the technical skill or the confidence to execute it at that moment in time. I worked it over so many times, but it never came together. It was such a struggle to let it go, but I finally had to face the fact that it wasn't working."

Harriet Smart

"Ideas don't work out; lots of them; all the time. But there'll be another one along in a minute and clinging to a feeble, sickly idea because you're afraid to let it go is a recipe for disaster."

Aline Templeton

Spotting that you have hit a blind alley is not always easy. Sometimes slow or even lack of progress is the main sign; fast and determined writing has more energy behind it. At other times there may be more subtle clues, such as a realisation that you are failing to daydream about particular characters; you may perhaps conclude that if they are not occupying your imagination, they are not 'real'. Others find that third-party judgement is really helpful here – an objective reader who will tell you honestly whether or not a character or situation is working. Discussing work with a third party can help you spot the level of determination you have to see the work through. Often, the very act of explaining how a difficult situation will resolve itself reveals inadequacies of plot or character.

What if other people don't like what you write?

This is a common problem. Whether or not you ask for feedback, other people may volunteer forceful opinions on the sort of book they think you should be writing, or not writing:

"I think I was 40 before I realised that almost every writer of fiction and poetry who has ever published a line has been accused by someone of wasting his or her God-given talent. If you write (or paint or dance or sculpt or sing, I suppose), someone will try to make you feel lousy about it, that's all. I'm not editorialising, just trying to give you the facts as I see them."

Stephen King (see bibliography)

"My first book was a big fat novel (about 300,000 words) so it took time for the feedback to trickle in. Some people found the book too heavy to hold. Other people gave a grudging, 'Well, it's not the sort of thing I usually read,' and then went on to say they had enjoyed it. Other people told me in no uncertain terms how much they had liked it and which bits had made them cry. There's a section when a child is drowned and one woman, a mother, said, 'You got the mother's reaction just right.' That was great."

Harriet Smart

"'Oh, you write THOSE kinds of books? Why do you want to do that when you're so intelligent?' Grrr. This is always said by people who don't write themselves, and they have no idea how much work it is to write ANY kind of book – nor what it's like to be proud of the achievement of having finished it and gotten it published.

I do write about sex but am clear that what I am writing about is my characters in a particular situation, not my husband and myself. You have to put yourself out of the picture, not think about what your mother will think, and get on with the plot."

Julie Cohen

"I have a love-hate relationship with customer reviews on Amazon, which I look at too regularly. You can't argue with readers. They are not critics; they have paid good money for your book; they are entitled to their opinion. This is marvellous when they're posting a positive review, four or five stars, but dispiriting when they hated the book and give it a one. This lowers the average rating, something you can do nothing about. I would personally never post a one-star review on Amazon. Once you've been on the other end of one and seen the permanent scar they leave, you'd think twice – unless you were a really horrible person!"

Andrew Collins

There are many instances of writers who become known for one type of book but long to write something else (Dorothy L Sayers is better known for her detective stories about Lord Peter Wimsey than her translation of Dante; Sir Arthur Conan-Doyle wanted to write serious history, not more adventures for Sherlock Holmes). Ultimately, the decision about what to write about must be the writer's, although this is often dictated by market forces (usually, how much you need the income).

Using stories that compromise others

"Writing is turning one's worst moments into money."

JP Donleavy (b1926), US novelist

Is there any limit to what you should write about? Is it your duty to raid your personal experiences for material, or can you only safely do this once the protagonists are dead? This is obviously down to the individual conscience, but many writers would claim that it is their *duty* to use what material they come across, even if in the process they embarrass their family and friends, because each human instance reveals truth. Some overcome their squeamishness about revealing personal information because through describing and interpreting it in their writing, the specific becomes general and part of a wider understanding of the human condition. This argument has also been used to justify writing about evil; without understanding, how can we try to prevent circumstances that produce it; or is it ever possible, or desirable, to do this?

One may argue that this distancing from the personal is similar to journalists being taught on professional courses that the story matters more than anything, even family loyalties, and insurance trainees being required to sell a policy to a family member or friend as part of their basic training.

For more practical guidance on matters such as libel/slander and litigation, the Society of Authors provides a series of short guides and will advise members on relevant contractual points that need attention.

Summary

Ultimately, what you decide to write about is your decision – or the decision of your subconscious. Whatever area you select, you will live with for a long time; bore your friends with details they might not wish to know; divert your family's travel plans with a need to visit specific locations; and fill your sleeping hours with related thoughts. Be sure it is an area you want to explore in such detail!

Questionnaire

Now turn to the questionnaire at the end of this book. Do you find yourself looking at situations you have lived through and thinking which words you would use to explain them to your friends? Do you update and improve on things you have talked about in order to make their description more effective, and to engage those listening to you more fully? Do you find yourself railing at pieces written by other writers because they have left things out and imagine how you would have shaped a piece on the same subject? Do you formulate in your head (but not always get down on paper) outlines for pieces that deal with key issues? Do you have ideas that you plan to turn into longer stories at some point in the future? Do other people find the things you talk or write about interesting? Do they ask you what happened next? Once you have thought about these issues, give yourself a mark out of ten for the resources you have at your disposal to write about.

7

How confident are you to present yourself as a writer?

There will be some who feel real distaste for this chapter, for which I apologise. In my defence I quote the experience of other published writers:

> "I am about to have my second book published; my first was last year. I have been writing for 25 years now. I found it interesting and awful to realise that perhaps having the ability to write well is perhaps the least important skill I needed in order to become a published writer. Nowadays, one must have the tenacity, originality and the ability to put oneself forward whatever the circumstances. If I had one piece of advice for beginners, it would be: learn the system."
>
> Molly Cutpurse

Writers write. They are experts in the selection and combination of words. It does not follow that they should also be articulate when spoken to or attractive to look at, in the same way that newsreaders are not necessarily tall, comics the life and soul of parties, and dress designers thrilled to run you up a little number at a moment's notice.

Yet in order to promote your writing career, it will help enormously if you are willing to be part of the marketing process, and on occasion to 'play the writer'.

Many writers resent this. They look back with nostalgia to a halcyon age when writers could leave it to their publishers to handle all the marketing, and they were judged on their work alone. Today, writers are increasingly required to turn strumpet: to appear at literary festivals and give readings; to agree to be interviewed by journalists and provide interesting quotes; to have their picture taken as a 'feature', with a controversial background, rather than the more familiar head-and-shoulders author portrait used on a book's back cover. Publishers want them to do this because free publicity in the media helps to sell books; journalists want them to take part because they tend to provide good copy. And actually, the halcyon age when authors did not have to take part in marketing may be much further back than you think:

> "Every great and original writer, in proportion as he is great and original, must himself create the taste by which he is to be relished."
>
> William Wordsworth (1770–1850)

How to boost your sense of yourself as a writer

"I think it helps to have a self-image or label for how you think about yourself. If you think 'I am a writer' it influences your behaviour. A writer writes, and everything they do, everybody they meet, all the places they visit have the potential to provide 'copy'."

Sheila Cornelius

For the yet-to-be published writer	For the published writer
Go to a writers' conference.	Offer to give a paper or presentation at a writers' conference. The organisers are often on the look-out for speakers, either as part of the main programme or at a fringe event. Supply the details of your titles in print to the organisers, who have usually sold the right to sell at the event to a local bookseller; better still, contact the bookseller direct. If you are selling your own books at an event, offer

For the yet-to-be published writer	For the published writer
	a discount for the duration but don't mention it too often – I know my own willingness to buy a speaker's book diminishes according to the number of times it gets mentioned.
Take a writing course.	Offer to tutor on a writing course. If they are already well served, offer to do a guest slot on one, talking about your experience of how to get published. You may not get paid but your experiences will be interesting to the audience and your morale will be boosted.
Browse in bookshops to see what is being published. It may give you ideas of gaps to fill or subjects to extend.	Offer to give a talk in a bookshop. Bookshops are trying to create a loyal clientele, who will come in and enjoy the 'buzz' on offer; it's a tangible way of keeping customers loyal rather than allowing them to drift off and purchase through 'impersonal' websites. As a consequence, several shops will offer to put on readings by both local and nationally known authors. You may have to provide the booze (which always helps attract an audience) but you get the chance to read aloud and to sell titles off the back of the event.

Develop eccentricities. Think about what helps you feel creative and become known for it – whether it is dressing in long, floaty clothes or wearing a panama hat. Beware of taking this too far, though: while eccentricities can make you memorable, they are best combined with an

For the yet-to-be published writer   For the published writer

attention to contractual detail. Douglas Adams may have made us smile when he commented on the whizzing sound deadlines make as they rush past, but in general:

"It isn't 'creative' or 'artistic' to be disorganised. It's simply irritating for all concerned with the complex process of publishing if you miss deadlines, give inaccurate references, or produce thousands of words more or less than agreed."

Hedi Argent

And Stephen King is very clear on whether or not writers need additional support:

"The idea that creative endeavour and mind-altering substances are entwined is one of the great pop-intellectual myths of our time ... Substance-abusing writers are just substances abusers ... Life is not a support-system for art. It's the other way around."

Enter a writing competition.

Offer to judge – or organise – a writing competition. Local papers love these, as they help boost a sense of local identity among their audience, as well as promoting the paper and boosting sales.

How to make yourself sound interesting to the rest of the world

There are many opportunities for writers to seek coverage for themselves; unfortunately, not all of these are based on an ability to write. The fact that you have a book coming out may attract the attention of features writers and gossip columnists – no other industry offers more opportunities for coverage (book review pages, features, gossip columns, news items). The trouble is – and this will really irritate many of you – the opportunities rise in proportion to the amount you will say about yourself that has nothing to do with the book.

Again, I doubt that this is anything completely new:

> "A reader seldom peruses a book with pleasure until he knows whether the writer or it be a black man or a fair man, of a mild or choleric disposition, married or a bachelor."
> Joseph Addison (1672–1719), English essayist, poet and statesman

In journalistic terms, what the media are looking for is 'pegs' – issues on which stories can be hung and around which ideas can cluster. What you provide will make it easier to make you sound interesting.

One important caveat: interest in you will be in proportion to how much you reveal about yourself; but the more you reveal about yourself, the more intrusive you will find the experience. And as the Roman poet Horace observed, "Once out, what you've said can't be stopped." It's possible for writers to be stuck with a sensational reputation because of their desperation for publicity. However persuasive journalists are in their attempt to encourage you to put 'your side of a story or issue', your interests are not identical. You may be wanting to put a point of view; they are trying to interest their readers, in the long-term hope of selling more papers. Journalists are ultimately responsible to the owners of their papers, not to those they write about.

Examples of facts/stories the media may find interesting

- What was your childhood like? The more controversial you can make it sound, the better. Did you move house three times before you were three (and what effect did this have on you?); do you still have two parents? Andrew Collins turned this on its head by trading on his stable and uneventful childhood, announcing it to be a desperate legacy for a potential writer in *Where Did It All Go Right?*

- Who are you married to; who do you have a relationship with? The more interesting/controversial, the better.

- What did you do in your youth that could now be highlighted? Youthful adventures can shed empathetic light on a character known for a more professional output. For example, Judy Garton-Sprenger, a well-known ELT author for Macmillan, recently told me that she had modelled for Dali in her youth – but had never told her publishers – perhaps because she worried it would diminish the seriousness with which they took her writing. Maybe this was the case at the beginning of her writing career, but now she is sufficiently well established for them to be delighted by this story. What glamour!

- What was your path to publication? Strewn with rejection letters or accepted first time round? Either can sound interesting. Stories of JK Rowling pushing her daughter around Edinburgh and stopping for coffee and to write when she fell asleep were very engaging.

- Where do you live and can we make that sound fascinating? What useful facts can you provide about the local area?

Remember that this information will be used to sell you – both within the publishing house at meetings about your book, and to the media. Your book *will* ride on the back of personal information that other people find fascinating. I am sorry if this undermines your faith in how book decisions are made (for more on this, see chapter 10 on publishing).

If you still find the whole process intolerable:
- Try to think of yourself as an object and describe yourself – it's much easier if you are not emotionally involved.

- Write with your tongue in your cheek; this always helps.

- Get a friend to help; what seems humdrum to you can be more interesting to others.

- Cultivate a reputation for inscrutability (although this is getting harder to do, as there are more and more writers, and quite a few have staked out this territory already).

- Consider attracting negative attention. Downright rudeness always makes for a good copy. Then, let those who come to interview you be surprised by how charming you are!

Some writers withhold key information because they are aware that they have strong material, which they may want to use themselves in the future. For example, Janet Street-Porter never talked to journalists about her difficult childhood and unusual mother. Rather than give away these gems to other writers, she kept them for her own autobiography, where they were revealed for the first time.

This process in practice
The author has three children.
Mary juggled writing with a permanent sense of stickiness, changing nappies and with vomit on her shoulder; the first draft of her book was completed while she had three children under five. There are many reports of agents receiving manuscripts that smelt of tobacco; she worried that hers would smell of Sudocream.

Martin Black works on the commodities exchange.
Martin Black trades in the food market, buying bananas from Trinidad while they are still green and ordering quantities of nutmeg that have not even yet been planted.

Jeremy is a teacher.
Jeremy had a very critical audience for his first reading: a class of 30 ten-year-olds who would have break (their favourite lesson) once the bell rang. His ability to hold their attention gave him the confidence to try and win over a publishing house.

Patronage

I love the elongated portrait art of the first half of the 20th century by artists such as Sir John Lavery and Etienne Drian.[1] In the National Portrait Gallery there hangs a wonderful portrait of King George V, Queen Mary and two of their children (the future Edward VIII and Princess Mary). I was listening to the Gallery's CD-Rom recently, which gives interesting snippets of information, and found out that the king and queen visited the studio late in

---

1 Favourite example in Leeds Castle, portrait of Lady Baillie, the last private owner of the castle and her daughters, Pauline and Susan.

the portrait's development, and there was a special space reserved for the king to paint on the picture himself. And once he had finished, the queen had a go too. A small painting-by-numbers section in the middle of a major commission. My immediate feeling was to wonder how the artist felt about this. Was it his idea? Did he feel patronised or celebrated? Did it help get him more commissions, or did he feel irritated by having to set up this artificial part of the composition, which probably had to be painted over afterwards?

Writers often have to hold their temper. People who are dismissive about your work may have sufficient power of patronage to make it foolish to alienate them. Others who have never read what you write can make sweeping judgements. And legacies of frustration can hang around for a very long time and then emerge in bitter book reviews; tit for tat.

The novice writer does well to build up some patronage – people who are willing to endorse what you have written. Quotations do not have to come from the famous (although this helps), but rather from the credible: thus, a novel for children endorsed by a parent and a child as well as a better-known name would impress a potential publisher or agent. You may be expected to think that your book is tremendous; third-party opinion is much more influential.

Also under patronage comes the flattering solicitation of your own opinion. Once you start to get known as a writer, other budding writers will feel that you have time to read, comment on and prepare for publication what they have in mind. On one level this is good; being asked for your support means that you are recognised. On the other hand, time is not infinitely expandable, and all such requests eat into your writing time. It also matters how the request is phrased. I get quite irritated by letters which assume, because I am writing, that I have time to do this. I commented on this to a writing friend who had just received the following, from someone she barely knows:

> "Over to you now. I can't go any further without professional input, and it's probably now time for you to send what I have drafted to some of your publishing contacts."

If someone does ask if they can send you stuff to look at, consider whether it's an area you are familiar with (can you give an opinion on science fiction if you never read any?) and what kind of feedback they are looking for (general encouragement, specific critique or details of which publisher to send it to?). In general, my advice is usually for the budding author to be clear about what kind of book they are writing, and who it is for, and to be familiar enough with bookshop stocking policy to know in which section it would be stocked. If they can describe a product the publisher can envisage existing, you are off to a good start. Buying a copy of the *Writers' & Artists' Yearbook* is a good investment for any writer.

More broadly, the very act of writing usually helps you understand yourself, and your situation, more fully – so in my opinion it is more useful to encourage people than to put them down. There is little point in making enemies: an over-frank response to someone's work, even if well intentioned, will almost certainly spill over into that person's attitude to your own books.

"Sharing your work is an act of great bravery. I have several times sent out stuff for comment and been very grateful for the feedback. If people don't want to comment, that's fine. What I find difficult to forgive is those who don't respond, and then come up with silly reasons why they did not have time to read the small chunk you sent them. It trivialises me and my work."

Doing an author event

Sooner or later the chance will occur for you to talk about yourself and your work. It may be to a special interest group, or to a school. Having longed for people to take an interest, the prospect can suddenly seem very daunting.[2] How do you gain the necessary confidence – or at least sound confident, even if you don't feel it?

2 Advice available from Catherine Dell; see useful contacts in the Appendix.

- Think about who is in the audience and why. Focusing on their expectations may help you to feel professional and contractual – and so to move beyond nerves.

- Find out all you can about what they want you to do. How long do they want you to talk for, and what kind of programmes have gone down well in the past? Prepare accordingly. William Hague's immense success as an after dinner-speaker has been much publicised lately. One of the reasons I have seen quoted for his popularity is the large amount of preparation he puts into finding out whom he is talking to; it is *not* the case that everyone gets the same material.

- Find out all you can about the venue: the sound quality, seating, heating (important for what to wear), and other facilities. Referring to these can make you sound really at home (e.g. 'I know we need to stop in time for the caretaker to lock the outer doors at 4.00 p.m., so let's make best use of our time together and get started.')

- Practise what you plan to say or read, preferably in front of kind friends who will give honest feedback. Time yourself.

- Relax your upper body. There are simple relaxation exercises and yoga positions that will help. Head for the loo and try them out there if you want privacy!

- Vary the delivery pace. Short extracts followed by longer, pausing for effect. In general, talk more slowly.

- Maintain eye contact with different parts of the audience so everyone feels included. Look up at regular intervals.

- I prefer to stand rather than sit, as it helps me project my voice and to feel 'in role'.

- Tell the person introducing you all the key points they should pass on; don't assume that they will do the research to find out about you, and remember – you are probably just one speaker out of many they have introduced. Being presented as you wish to be seen is important. The words of the introducer will be ringing in the audience's ears and will colour the beginning of your presentation.

If you worry that your social skills have atrophied from sitting too long on your own over a typewriter or in front of a computer, practise talking on the way there, or get a friend to give you a 'mock' interview. Listen to other writers being interviewed and observe how it's done. If you feel nervous, remind the audience that writers are mainly known for their writing, not their talking. The audience is on your side and wants you to do well.

When your friends and family are present ...

It can be tricky, when giving readings and leading workshops, to deal with members of the audience whom you already know. Many writers have alternative versions of themselves that they parade on public occasions, and these may differ markedly from the day-to-day reality.

I work regularly as a trainer within the publishing industry, teaching people the skills I needed when I worked in the marketing department. At a time when my children were really small, there was a huge difference between my day job at home, and the professional trainer I liked to appear to be. As I drove from Kingston to Wandsworth, I would feel myself morphing between the two roles. Dressing up for the occasion always helped, as did tuning the radio into something uplifting.

If you are asked to give a presentation to an audience that may include several people who know you well, the comments of this actor may be helpful:

"I am aware that actors describing how their craft works can sound very self-indulgent, but here goes. When you are on the stage, you have to develop a sort of schizophrenia to deal with the attention of the audience. So whereas you, the actor, may notice a familiar face in the audience, and make that momentary recognition, the character you are playing will not, and you have to move on; the distraction has to be temporary – otherwise you would not be able to do it. It can be hard if the critics have either liked or disliked a particular point in the play, because as you approach it, it no longer feels part of the play. It is in danger of becoming an isolated moment in which you become self-conscious, saying in effect, 'Here comes the bit they like', which of course can ruin your performance. I try not to read the critics until after the play has finished, but of course that demands immense self-restraint.

Of course after the play is over, curiosity takes over and it is wonderful to know if friends liked it. I can take negative feedback, and quite often I think they are right."

Summary

This chapter may well have irritated you. Why should writers have to 'strut their stuff' in the public arena when they are happiest with pen in hand, in glorious isolation? Why should what you look like or how well you talk be important considerations to the agent or publisher who is taking you on? Remember, though, that there is only one thing worse than the wrong sort of attention, and that is being ignored.

> "There is nothing more dreadful to an author than neglect, compared with which, reproach, hatred and opposition are names of happiness; yet this worst, this meanest fate, everyone who dares to write has reason to fear."
>
> Samuel Johnson[3]

Questionnaire

Now turn to the questionnaire. When you answer this question, you have to think seriously about whether or not you are willing to play a part in the promotion of your book. Will you agree to be interviewed by media you do not read, or worse still, media you despise? Will you answer inane questions from members of the audience which make it plain that they have not been listening to your previous three answers to the same question, and have never read one of your books? Will you give readings and chat charmingly to the host who confesses before you start that they never read 'your kind of writing'? Now give yourself a mark out of ten for your willingness to play the role of the writer.

3 Quoted in *The Courage to Write*, Ralph Keyes (see bibliography).

8

How positively do you respond to rejection?

"Creating a story that lives on the page, characters that live within it, takes time, endless practice, a measure of luck, and also a sort of pathological refusal to be put off by failure."

Lynn Freed (see bibliography)

This book is about how to get published, so a whole chapter on how you respond to rejection may seem unduly negative. I would argue however that it is important to address realities. However much you want to write a book, there will be plenty of people only too willing to dissuade you from trying. Their negative input can come at all stages, from rubbishing the very idea that you have either the time or the talent to write, to dismissing your completed manuscript. What the determined writer has to do is distinguish between useful feedback and useless distraction. How much you want to get there will very substantially influence your chances of arrival.

In one area at least, writers do tend to be optimists. We all know that publishers and agents *do* get it wrong; they turn down what go on to be bestsellers from other houses; they fail to spot genius when it appears before them, simply because they do not understand that it has genuine market appeal or merit rather than just being 'different' and therefore instantly dismissable. There are the much-repeated stories of authors who have amassed multiple rejection letters, only to go on and be successful. And all would-be writers know that *Harry Potter* was turned down by a host of better-known publishing firms than Bloomsbury – Puffin included.

There are two important caveats to this optimism. The first is that such stories stand out because they are unusual. Agents and publishers are experienced, and their professionalism is often completely underrated by authors. While they cannot entirely predict the taste of the reading public – because public taste is essentially fickle – they get it right more often than they get it wrong. Authors also underrate publishers' commitment. Talk to any publisher about their regrets and they will outline the stories of talented writers whose work has never taken off to the extent they hoped it would. Believe me, publishers are not in it for the money.

The second caveat is that the determination of the author plays a key part in these much-told 'publisher incompetence' stories. In every case where an author is rejected but goes on to be successful, the key ingredient in the reversal has been author determination; the 'pathological refusal to be put off by failure' described by Lynn Freed above.

What is rejection within a writing context?

A rejection from a publishing house or by a literary agency is a specific decision from one individual at a particular time, based on prevailing market and cultural conditions. It means that the particular person you approached – or the person who handled your manuscript/idea/submission on their behalf – does not, at the moment, want to take on this particular proposal. It is not a rejection of:

- You as a writer.
- You as a person.
- Any books you might write in the future.
- You as a candidate for this particular publishing house or agency, as other people within the same firm may feel differently.

"Bear in mind that the agent or publisher wants to find books which will sell to the reading public in the immediate future. So don't feel that rejection necessarily means you can't write. You may have written the wrong kind of book at the wrong time, and fashions in publishing are always changing, so what was the wrong book this year might be the right book two or three years down the line."

Margaret James

You should also understand that initial acceptance or rejection is one stage in an ongoing critical process. Very few writers get taken on immediately, unless it is for reasons other than their writing – i.e. they are well known in other fields and so their promotion as writers can build on their established celebrity. Most titles are accepted on the basis that they will need to be revised, and the process of preparing a manuscript for publication involves endless critical assessment and improvement.

> "The first time I had a book accepted I thought that was it, my work was being appreciated and wasn't I the clever one? I was deeply upset when my editor suggested, or really demanded, amendments, additions or cuts on nearly every page. Twelve books later I know that my editor is my best publishing friend, and I await her comments eagerly to shape my final draft – but I have also gained enough confidence to know that she isn't always right. So, don't take it personally when your editor sends back your precious manuscript with red marks all over it."
>
> Hedi Argent

> "'I've always liked editorial feedback and still do; it helps to switch me into reader mode, which is difficult. After all, I know what I meant to say. It's difficult to work out whether that comes off the page without someone else's reaction to bounce off."
>
> Jenny Haddon

Indeed, the whole process of having interest from an agency, and being asked for revisions, can end in tears:

> "I thought, somehow, that I had crafted a masterpiece. It felt so easy, so perfect, that I was convinced the publishing world would be swept away. I had an agent who had indicated she wanted to sign me up and an admiring gaggle of youngsters who seemed to enjoy the work. My third-age career was mapped out. I packed the manuscript off to the agent and waited for the cheque. 'Not bad,' came the eventual reply. 'Just rewrite the first half and we will take another look.' Two rewrites later I found the returned manuscript and my first rejection letter waiting on the doorstep. I couldn't believe

it. 'But you said you wanted me,' I bleated. 'Our readers disagreed with our assessment. Sorry,' came the reply. My arrogance was punctured but the air was leaking out slowly. What do they know, I thought. I sent it to another agent and was immediately taken up. The puncture was mended.

My new agent set about marketing the book and sent it to four publishers. The responses were so universally negative that we decided to shelve the first book and start another. The slow leak was back. I began to understand that this would not be the breeze I had thought it would be. Being self-critical was the hardest thing. I felt an artist's pride in my creation and was unable to see the flaws. I am not, in general, either arrogant or vain but I'm afraid that I was and still am guilty of both sins when it comes to my writing. I find it almost impossible to detach myself from the creative process and look at the novel as a reader. I have to rely on others for that and I am learning the hard way to respect their judgements."

John Whitley

I reprint this at length because it contains such a growing self-knowledge. While maintaining his determination to get into print, John charts the process of accepting viewpoints other than his own.

"If you are going to want people to like your work, then you have to accept it when they don't. Inviting people's opinions on whether your writing is good enough to be published and paid for inevitably means there will be people who do not think it is good enough.

Working as a sports journalist I have developed a pretty thick skin and I think that stood me in good stead for when publishers have rejected book proposals. It is frustrating, but there's no point wallowing in self-pity. If a publisher rejects your script, take on board what they have to say and move on."

Adam Powley

"If reactions are honest (and they often aren't!) then they should be mixed. No one can write a book that everyone loves – all I ever hope is that SOME people will love it. I like to provoke strong reactions, and that's usually what I get, one way or the other. No one has ever said 'your book was OK'!"

Nicola Morgan

Minimising the chance of rejection

Here are some basic tips to minimise the chance of rejection *before* you submit your work for review by others.

Is it any good?

> "Learn to write well, or not to write at all."
> John Sheffield (1648–1721), English poet and statesman

Every writing competition will eventually find the judges commenting that, although the standard of some of the submissions was very high, there were some truly dreadful entries, where one wondered how the writer could have thought their work suitable for publication. Just because you have finished a piece of writing and have an envelope and stamp to hand, it does not mean you have written something worth reading by other people. Take on board the advice in this book, and others, on appraising the standard of your own work. Be honest with yourself.

> "What is written without effort is in general read without pleasure."
> Samuel Johnson

Are you sending it off at the right time?

'The right time' here means both in the evolution of your writing, and of yourself as a writer. Most writers want feedback and contact, and it can be so tempting to fire off your newly compiled synopsis or completed manuscript to someone who is bound to love it. The trouble is that few of us get it absolutely right first time, and in your haste to share, you could be seriously compromising your future chance of publication. So sit on it. Re-read it a week later; Stephen King recommends six weeks later. Get a friend to read it; ask an opinion from someone who will be objective, but not crushing.

> "Everything that gets sent into us gets read, and we try to provide feedback. But I often feel people waste our time. Many times I have found myself saying to a writer, 'I found the characters really boring,

I just wasn't interested in them as people.' And the response I get if I say this is invariably 'Yes, they are quite boring aren't they?' Don't waste our time or yours. If something is not ready or right for submission, don't submit until it is."

Kate Rowland, Creative Director of New Writing at the BBC

"Rejection slips are nasty, cold little things and have a dampening effect on your spirit. There seems no point in dampening the flame of your creativity before it's had a chance to start burning properly. So unless you're sure that even the curtest rejection slip won't stop you writing, wait a while before you send anything out."

Kate Grenville (see bibliography)

Othere people's timing – will they look at it?

Are you sending your at a time when your intended recipient can look at it? If you are approaching people likely to attend Book Fairs, avoid October (Frankfurt – preparation and follow-up) and March (London – ditto). On the other hand, these *can* be good times at which to send things, if people are not attending. An agent of my acquaintance recently told me that she was not attending Frankfurt and took a week's holiday, on the grounds that 'no one would notice she was missing'. And of course, for publishers who have not had the chance to attend, finding something back home to enthuse about is a good way of dealing with their own sense of rejection!

Similarly, whereas the pre-Christmas rush can be a poor time to get noticed, the period between Christmas and New Year, and the early days of January, can be quiet times to look at a manuscript. It's a good idea to check (without harassing anyone!) that your would-be recipient is in the office/still employed at the time you plan to send your big idea off. Remember too that publishers work far in advance – they will be asking themselves whether potential readers will still be interested in the subject/theme of your writing in two years' time. If it is *too* topical they may feel it will date too quickly to be publishable, in which case you might be better off trying to get it published as an article in a magazine rather than as a book.

Are you sending it to the right place/person?

Have you done some basic homework on the publisher/agent you are approaching? What kind of books do they handle, and how would your proposal fit with the rest of their list? The most recent edition of the *Writers' & Artists' Yearbook* will give you the name of the person commissioning in each area of a publisher's list, but don't forget that the book is out of date from the moment it goes to print, so send an email to your proposed contact and ask if they are indeed the right person to approach. Email rather than ring – it's less invasive and it will create an impression of you as a professional person who values everyone's time, your own included.

For more information on researching/approaching publishers and agents, refer to Chapter 10.

> "Don't stalk editors – this will only put them off your work. Instead, before you submit, do the research on precisely which authors and books the editor/publisher favours."
>
> Submissions editor

Do you look professional?

It is hard to say this often enough: *you don't get a second chance to make a first impression*. What you send should be error-free and clean. A tired-looking manuscript carries the subliminal message that it has been oft-rejected. There is more advice on what to send and how in chapter 10 on understanding the publishing profession.

Are you really prepared for the publishing world?

This is a tricky paragraph to write, because by background I am a publisher, but the publishing world can seem distinctly hostile to outsiders – authors included. Publishers and agents (many of whom used to be publishers) ooze confidence and self-knowledge. Whether or not they are in a position to make a qualified assessment or a rational judgement, they appear impelled to sound as if they do. From receptionists upwards, they are confident and even dismissive. They tend to have posh names and posh voices.

Once a year the book world gathers for the annual London International Book Fair, usually held at Olympia. All attendees at

the Fair have the chance to specify how they want to be cate-
gorised on their name badge (publisher, bookseller, agent, etc.).
Having held various jobs within the publishing industry over the
years, I have experimented by identifying myself variously, and am
convinced that the label 'author' on your name badge leads most
commonly to averted eyes. Publishers, when grouped together, see
authors as a nuisance. Those whom they want to be there (their
hot prospects or existing bestsellers) have been asked to make
special appearances; others are likely to be bothersome. I have often
winced to hear the dismissive way in which authors who approach
publishers' stands are dealt with; often, the more regional the
accent, the more instant the brush-off. Manchester author Livi
Michael sent her first novel to an agent and the response was:

> "I couldn't imagine anyone being interested in the lives of four
> women living on a council estate in the north of England."
>> (The novel, *Under a Thin Moon*, was sent to another agent who
>> had two offers of publication for it. It was eventually published by
>> Secker & Warburg and went on to win the Arthur Welton award)

Be prepared. Whatever the reasons for this – and many authors
have speculated that deep down, publishers are often jealous of
authors and feel they would make a much better job of the writing
if only they had the time – it is a world in which you need to be
strong in order to survive. Remember that, to quote Gilbert and
Sullivan, 'Faint heart never won fair lady.'

How patient are you?
Don't start scanning the post for a response a week after you send
your material off. Reading something with a view to publication
takes time, and the feedback you get (even if it is a rejection) will
be more valuable, the more thought that has been put into it.

> "Our firm gets around 2,000 submissions a year, hence the delays
> in getting a response, or even getting only a cursory impersonal
> one. It takes time and engagement to read what has been sent in,
> so don't rush us."
>> Submissions editor

147

How to respond to a rejection

Have you been rejected?

It may seem strange, but spotting a rejection letter is sometimes tricky. They tend to be full of careful phrases that can make it questionable whether or not the writer has in fact been rejected. Canongate Books Ltd recently received a confused letter back from an author who said, 'You seem to like my book so much I can't see why you have rejected it.' The response of the publisher was that often, submissions may show promise of a talented writer-to-be, even if the book in question is not publishable; therefore, it is important to leave the door ajar, rather than slam it in a rejected writer's face.

What does a rejection letter look like? Sometimes they are brief in the extreme – a compliments slip or a standard form with an illegible signature at the bottom. Some houses send a standard letter, which may include some of the following phrases:

- Does not suit our list as it is currently developing
- Your idea, while attractive ...
- Insufficient commercial appeal
- The market is difficult and it would be hard to do it justice
- Please feel free to approach other publishers
- Wishing you every success ...

Please note that, tempting though it is to read things into rejection letters, just because they 'wish you every success on your path to publication' does not imply their unshakeable confidence that you will get there. You really don't want to develop a correspondence that is likely to be irksome to the recipient, or to create difficulties for yourself with a particular individual in the future. (Publishing staff tend to job-hop, so that someone you have fallen out with is likely to crop up in another key position in future.) Remember too that those you are approaching circulate within the industry fairly regularly, thus most publishers' rejection letters are similar. On no account quote from one rejection letter when resubmitting your material to another publisher. If you tell them what another publisher said. you are telling them that you have already been rejected.

> "In the recent film *Sideways*, there is a wonderful but awful scene when the hero is told by his agent that the publisher he had been counting on has passed on his book. The words the agent uses were virtually identical to ones used by my agent at one point. A real 'Omigod' moment. Do they have a little book of stock phrases they keep by the phone, I wondered?"
>
> Harriet Smart

Other authors come to feel that the careful phrases just waste everyone's time. As an author now self-publishing wrote:

> "If only those I contacted had said, 'Your book is good, but you are over 70 and I suspect this is the only book you will write. In those circumstances I'm afraid no publisher will want to invest in you and so no agent (who all know about publishers) will take you on for the same reason.' This may not have reflected terribly creditably on the publishing world, but it might have saved me three more years of heartache and expense. Each submission costs at least £6 by way of postage – there and back – which is nearly £200 down the drain for starters. Also I get no younger."
>
> Judge Martin Tucker

How it feels

> "How does it feel when I get a rejection letter? Worthless. Untalented. Ready to go and get a proper job. The important thing is not to take it personally. They are not rejecting you or your ability, just that particular project. That is easy to say, of course, because when the knife goes in, it goes in deep.
>
> Take comfort that you are not the only one. Then if you are feeling strong enough (maybe a little later) dust yourself down, and see what that rejection is really telling you. Is there a way you can turn this project round, make it more viable, more marketable? What other options have you got? To use a film reference, be Scarlett O'Hara in that vegetable patch."
>
> Harriet Smart

"The first effect of a rejection letter is like sexual rejection, only worse. I lick my wounds for anything up to 24 hours, then try to work out why it was rejected and learn from the experience. Never throw any completed proposal away. What I can't cannibalise, I can learn from."

Jenny Haddon

"Actually I feel sick, depressed and angry, but not surprised. I try to be practical about it and move quickly on to the next outlet, but it's never easy. I don't think I'll ever stop feeling that way."

Anne Brooke

"I could paper my house with 21 years of rejection letters and every one stung me at the time. Luckily now I don't get them, as everything I do is commissioned. I have no tips for dealing with them, except as with all insect stings, say ouch and then move on."

Nicola Morgan

"Toughen up. It's not personal. Anyone who tells you he/she hasn't had rejections is LYING. Writing is hugely subjective. If you aren't getting at least one rejection a week (for something) then you aren't trying hard enough. Look at the book review pages and see how many published books – which have been accepted, edited, paid for some by well-known names – are scathingly criticised. If that reviewer had been in a critical position earlier in the process, the book might have been rejected."

Anne Sebba

Extracting the positive message from rejection

Each rejection offers a clue to future acceptance. If you get a standard letter or a compliments slip, then you can be pretty sure that your submission was not interesting to the publisher you sent it to. A slightly longer letter, which refers to particular incidents of plot, character or market, shows that more trouble has been taken and may yield further information.

When submitting short stories very early in his career, Stephen King charts the progress of moving from a rejection slip that said only. 'Don't staple manuscripts. Loose pages plus paperclip equals correct way to submit copy,' to, 'This is good. Not for us, but good. You have talent. Submit again.' He put all the rejection slips on a nail on his bedroom wall and the more encouraging spurred him on, although he confesses that 'when you're still too young to shave, optimism is a perfectly legitimate response to failure'.

"Rejections hurt, although I've trained myself to see the positive in them. I never would have understood the idea of a 'good' rejection before I started trying to get published! I never argued my case after receiving a rejection, but I have rung the editor to ask for further clarification. I'm a little embarrassed I did that now, though."

Julie Cohen

"Working as I do in radio and television, I have learned to live with rejection. It's par for the course. In 2005, I had a sitcom rejected twice by the BBC after putting in a lot of work on a treatment and two full scripts. I made a pilot documentary for BBC1 with BBC Bristol and even though we were all delighted with the finished product, it was turned down. As I say, it's part of the job in TV. You deal with it by using it as an opportunity for reflection: do I really want to do this? (Whether it's write scripts for TV, present programmes or write books.) Rejection makes me stronger. The day a rejection makes me feel like jacking it in is the day to jack it in. All the best writers have dealt with rejection."

Andrew Collins

"Read carefully any hand-written notes – these are your best tips for improvement. Tick them off your spreadsheet of submissions, take a deep breath and move on."

Anne Brooke

"How I feel when the rejection arrives depends on the rejection letter. If it's clear the book isn't right for that particular editor or agent but they say nice things about it otherwise, or encourage me to send other work to them, I'm quite content. If it's a 'form' rejection letter, that's more upsetting – but maybe it's just not right for them. Just about every good book has been rejected several times before being published, it's just part of the process."

Anne Rooney

> "There are lots of reasons for rejection, only some of which I can do anything about – it's a terrible idea and/or a terrible book; it's a good idea imperfectly realised; it's a good idea whose time hasn't come yet (that's the only one where I would try to argue a case); the publisher's risk-reward ratio is hopeless – e.g. a first novel of half a million words would cost a fortune to produce and almost certainly couldn't make any money. The other reasons are all about what agents and/or publishers have already got on their books, believe they can sell, and like, for God's sake."
>
> Jenny Haddon

> "Rejections are painful but I kept them all, and if any of them offered me any helpful advice, which many of them did, I wrote back and thanked them for taking the time to do so. I also never sat back to see what would happen to the book I had sent out, but instead started another one."
>
> Trisha Ashley

Whatever sort of rejection you get, the best advice is to do nothing straight away – although it is tempting to write an instant rebuttal – and then analyse it in the cold light of day. Resist the temptation to see rejection as the product of conspiracy or malevolence. Don't forget that the people you are approaching are professionals who are receiving a huge number of other submissions. What you sent in will have been seen in that context, it is unlikely to be personal spite. Some would-be authors set little challenges to those reviewing their work:

> "I knew he had not read it because I placed a hair between pages 200 and 201 and it was still there when the manuscript was returned."

But most of us can tell from the first few pages of a book whether or not we are likely to enjoy it, so perhaps would not feel the need to plough on! Publishers' livelihoods depend on getting it right most of the time; even more so for agents, whose income comes from the authors they choose to represent. Above all:

"Don't let the search for a publisher inhibit your drive to write. Enjoy writing, or struggle to write the next book, while the rejection slips for your masterpiece keep coming through the letterbox."

Hedi Argent

Querying a rejection

You may also want to consider whether rejection is an opportunity to further explain your proposal to the publisher or agent. Be *very* careful here; the threshold at which people express annoyance seems to be getting lower all the time. I shared a platform with someone who recently announced how irritated she got by emails acknowledging emails, which has always seemed rather a helpful practice to me. You *really* don't want to develop a correspondence that is likely to be irksome to the recipient – but if you believe they have missed a key point, think of it as a retrial on the basis of new evidence rather than a chance to debate each point *ad infinitum*. It is easier to do this with non-fiction than with fiction:

"I once rejected a non-fiction title and gave specific reasons for doing so. The authors contacted me and made several good points about the market and the particular differences they were seeking to offer. They asked if we could meet and I agreed. When we met I listened carefully and I eventually thought they were right. I subsequently used their arguments in the presentation I made to colleagues about the book. We published it. I would point out, however, that this doesn't happen very often – normally a rejection is final."

Jenny Ridout, Senior Commissioning Editor, A&C Black

"The last time, I had submitted a commissioned piece for a journal and, thinking it was the best I had ever written (a danger sign, I realise now), was shocked when the editor said that he felt it wasn't up to standard and he wasn't sure if he could use it. Luckily, he was a very astute and supportive editor and we worked through the issues, but there was a great deal of screaming on my part, I'm ashamed to say. However, although I allowed some cuts, I did argue my case in a way that ensured the piece was not changed wholesale, and it was still run in the end – in fact, being quoted in many newspapers and even an academic paper! (Though, perhaps that's more due to his patience and intelligence than mine ...)

Generally, though, I don't bother arguing. Either an editor is kind enough or has enough time to give you some constructive criticisms, or they're not. Generally, they don't. Like most other writers, I have one less skin than everyone else, and dwell on the stupidest, silliest things for days on end."

Sunil Badami

"I would never argue the case after rejection. If they don't want it, you're not going to change their mind, and in any case, you'll only come across as needy. (Having been a commissioning editor on magazines is helpful. I've been on the other side, dealing with unsolicited articles and letters from would-be writers. If you're interested, you're interested. A follow-up call used to rub me up the wrong way!)"

Andrew Collins

"I don't get rejection letters. I've never had one. But if I did, I wouldn't waste my time arguing with it. If someone doesn't like your book, what are you going to say? 'Well you should!' The thing to do would be to feel sorry for this person of lamentably poor taste, and send your masterpiece somewhere else while busily writing the next one."

Philip Pullman

How to keep your morale up after rejection

"There's no mystery about why writers so often respond to any whisper of criticism with a spirited self-defence. It's not their writing that they feel is being picked at, but their souls."

Ralph Keyes (see bibliography)

The problem with rejection is that it is usually more than the book idea or sample of writing that is rejected. We ourselves feel rejected along with our manuscripts, and this hurts. Now is the time to take refuge in what else we have achieved:

- Build a file of positive things to look through every now and again. I have one on my desk and it includes feedback, thank-you letters, copies of articles I have had printed, and good reviews of my work. I find a quick glance through every now and again very uplifting.

- Most things look better if you are fit. Exercise helps.

- Do interesting things. Plan a social life around which to construct a life. (Is it just me, or do all writers hate surprise parties? I want to be able to look forward to the experience, think about who will come and get on with whom, and then slowly digest the experience afterwards. Surprise parties give me no writerly chance to explore all this.)

- Describe the experience to a friend. Most problems diminish when shared, and sharing the experience of rejecting the rejection can feel good (you can come back to it later to consider any constructive message that may be absorbed).

"File your rejection letters so that when your book is a bestseller, you can humiliate the people who were foolish enough to reject it. The more you get, the better your chance of publishing a great collection of rejection letters later."

Anne Rooney

- Look like you are successful. People take you at your own estimation. Success breeds success, and the chances are, if you look like you are successful, what you seek will follow. An example sticks in my mind from when I was still at school, when I had a summer job waitressing in a local restaurant. Most mornings, the lady whose restaurant it was – and after whom it was named – would head off into town to buy items from the market or flowers. I began by wondering why she had to go shopping so often – would it not be more effective to rationalise the plans and do it once a week? I soon realised it was part of her marketing strategy. She would go at different times of the day, but even when just wandering down the high street she always dressed for the occasion. We would see her arrive in jeans but before leaving the premises she always put on make-up, tied her hair up in a jaunty ponytail and sprayed on some perfume. She went out looking pleased to meet people and I am sure that extra business followed.

So, when you are going to a meeting, or to a book fair, look like you mean business. Publishers are looking for authors who are promoteable and saleable, and presentation matters hugely.

"The more powerfully you speak, the more you will be a force in the world around you. People who display an inner strength are treated differently from those who come across as weak."

Susan Jeffers (see bibliography)

"Keep looking tanned, live in an elegant building (even if you're in the cellar), be seen in smart restaurants (even if you nurse one drink), and if you borrow, borrow big."

Aristotle Onassis, referring to the secret of success
(*The Times*, 15th August, 1986)

Other sources of critical appraisal for your work

Learn to be self-critical

One of the most important assets possessed by any writer is balanced self-criticism.

"In the long run, it is your taste and your judgement that must carry you over the pitfalls, and the sooner you educate yourself into being all things to your writing-character, the better your prospects are."

Dorothea Brande

Sometimes this is best achieved through distance in time, putting your work to one side and coming back to it later; at other times, by trying to put yourself in the frame of mind of the reader, and coming to it afresh:

"I am my own best critic. I know if something's good or if it's just filler. I often print chapters out and take them with me on the train. Away from the computer, a hard copy, set in an attractive typeface that's small enough to look like the page of a book – that's the final test. If I like it on the train, it's finished."

Andrew Collins

"It's important to develop that little scarry callous on your writing hand, ensuring that you can keep criticisms objective and the work a little distant. Especially when you're a young, emerging writer who gets more rejections than established ones! I've found the more I separate myself from my work, the easier it is to deal with rejection and disappointment, and easier to work out the problems that the work might have – however (yet another contradiction) it is also important to trust your gut, and even if the work isn't published or publishable now, it may well be in a while – though whether that's a few months or years, who could say? Hope springs eternal ..."

Sunil Badami

"As to responses, well, they varied widely but in different ways were responding to the same failings. I came away with a much clearer sense of how I'd make the next one different and better – on my own terms as well as theirs.

And now, having been brought to a much harder, more critical frame of mind by the responses, I do wonder if some well-known authors would have had some later works published if they weren't so popular already. I'm sure if an *ingénu* had turned up with JM Coetzee's *Elizabeth Costello* or Annie Proulx's *That Old Ace In The Hole* they'd have been dismissed with a stern lecture on the relative commercial values of plot and fine prose."

Bernard Lyall

Being self-critical also starts from an understanding that it is *you* who needs to think about change – or sticking with it – rather than looking at others to change their attitudes. As Franklin Covey says in *The Seven Habits of Highly Effective People*:

"Look at the word responsibility – 'response-ability' – the ability to choose your response. Highly proactive people recognise that responsibility. They do not blame circumstances, conditions, or conditioning for their behaviour. Their behaviour is a product of their own conscious choice, based on values, rather than a product of their conditions, based on feeling."

"The fountain of content must spring up in the mind, and he who hath so little knowledge of human nature as to seek happiness by changing anything but his own disposition, will waste his life in fruitless efforts and multiply the grief he proposes to remove."

Samuel Johnson (1709–84)

Feedback from friends and colleagues

The advantage is that such advice tends to be cheap and available; the main disadvantage, that you may not get an honest answer:

"Whenever you ask someone to offer an opinion on your work, you must always think of all the reasons why they might not give an objective answer."

Nicholas Allan

Perhaps your friend or colleague is over-busy (and hence keen to say whatever they think you would like to hear, as quickly as possible, so as to move on to deal with the rest of their priorities). Perhaps they have a genuine desire to please you, or are jealous or polite (even though they hate what you have provided), or simply lack interest in (or comprehension of) your subject matter.

If you do decide to ask your friends for feedback, be specific about why you are doing it and what you are looking for. Are you seeking:

- Affirmation and reassurance?
- New ideas?
- Criticism?
- Practical feedback (does the ending work; do the characters feel real)?
- Comments on any important missing details?

Be clear about what you want to achieve – and do remember to say thank you. Reading work carefully in order to provide feedback takes time and effort, and may give rise to considerable angst if the friend reading it has to worry about how to be diplomatic!

Paying for feedback

Another way of getting feedback – without the time-consuming and socially awkward process of asking others to do you a favour, and then trying to decode their responses – is simply to pay for it. There are now several agencies offering expert guidance on how to improve a manuscript. The best known of these, The Literary Consultancy (TLC), was established by Rebecca Swift in 1986 (see appendix for details). While serving a useful apprenticeship as an editor in publishing, Becky found that providing detailed feedback to authors on why their manuscripts were not publishable, was not appreciated by those she worked for. She was told firmly: 'Our job is to spend time on what we are publishing, not on what we will not be publishing.' Her response was to set up The Literary Consultancy, where she could provide a higher level of feedback, in return for payment:

> "We offer, for a fee, professional, detailed, objective attention to manuscripts before they are submitted – or resubmitted – to publishers and agents. Alternatively, if a manuscript is not ready to send out, nor ever likely to be, we will do our best to be constructively candid."

One huge advantage of such a service is that criticism is detailed and *devoted just to your book*. As a friend wrote, of the recent experience of going to a counsellor:

> "One of the things I found hardest to get used to about counselling was the concentration on *me*. Having been nicely brought up, that you should engage others in talk rather than seek to hog the conversation, it was strange to find that everything revolved around me, there was no requirement for me to ask her what kind of a week she had had."

Instructing a literary consultant is like paying for counselling on your manuscript. It's one-to-one from an experienced person, concentrating solely on you. This is good value for money.

Creative Writing courses

A common method of working within many MA programmes is to encourage students to read their work aloud to others. Dorothea Brande described this as a 'thoroughly pernicious practice'. Arguably, it is always easier to criticise than to create, and she worried that such a method released unhealthy responses in students:

> "They seem to need to demonstrate that, although they are not yet writing quite perfectly themselves, they are able to see all the flaws in a story which is read to them, and they fall upon it tooth and fang."

Stephen King agrees that:

> "It's always easier to kill someone else's darlings than it is to kill your own."

Mick Stephens, who runs Kingston University's MA in Creative Writing sees 'peer-driven critiques as quite simply one of the most important parts of the MA experience'; and those running the MA in Creative Writing at the University of East Anglia regard the ability to take part in such seminars so beneficial that they highlight the possible impact in their admissions advice to prospective students:

> "The selection of candidates is based on submission of a portfolio of recent work and on interview. Applicants are assessed on the quality and potential of the work they submit with their application (a maximum of 5,000 words or up to 20 pages of poetry, or up to 30 pages of dramatic script/screenplay). We also attempt to choose those who would benefit from – rather than be damaged or deterred by – the intensive discussion of their own work in an environment which is both creative and critical. This means that temperamentally one needs a degree of endurance, resilience and willingness to face criticism."

It is *how* that criticism is delivered which makes the difference:

"Offering criticism of another's writing can be a precarious affair; listening to criticism can be downright disastrous. Many first-time participants in writing workshops clam up, or even stop writing altogether, because of the criticism of tutors and fellow writers, even if this criticism happens to be to the point, constructive and carefully delivered. Listening too reverently to misguided criticism, on the other hand, can lead to the jettisoning of a perfectly good idea."

Richard Aczel, *The Creative Writing Handbook* (see bibliography)

"For most people, writing seems almost an extension of their person. Criticise it and you criticise them; insult it and they suffer hurt; dismiss it and they are devastated. Writing is a material manifestation of the very processes of thought; and in our essential selves, we are what we think."

Beth S Neman, *Teaching Students to Write* (see bibliography)

While feedback which shames and ridicules can in no way be condoned, encouraging feedback with attention to the text can be very motivating.

How to give feedback yourself

Once you have had a measure of success in writing, you will find that other people approach you for feedback on their ideas and style. The following tips may be helpful:

1 Listen carefully first. Diagnose before you advise, and don't rush the response. Giving feedback is about someone else, not you.

"Most people do not listen with the intent to understand; they listen with the intent to reply. They're either speaking or preparing to speak. They're filtering everything through their own paradigms, reading their autobiography into other people's lives."

Franklin R Covey (see bibliography)

2 Criticism should be given in the context of having bothered to write at all. A piece of writing is always bigger than we are – so don't make the person whose work you are reviewing feel that they have wasted their time.

3 Think about the person who will be receiving your feedback. How much can they take? How important will your feedback be to their decision to carry on writing? Be careful! If the person feels that *they* are being rejected, they will be unable to act on the criticism.

4 What you suggest should respond to the author's context and intentions. Don't criticise a modern romance for not being as good as Jane Austen. Advice that cannot be put into practice is useless.

5 The critic and author should be equals; being asked to critique something does not involve a moral or social superiority.

6 Start with the positive. Most of us can cope with criticism if it is heralded by something – anything – that the critic liked first.

7 Don't try to impose a solution. Outline a problem by all means, but the decision to change course must be the writer's and not the critic's.

8 All critical suggestions must be supported by detailed reference to the text; spontaneous and sweeping generalisations are unhelpful.

Summary

It seems to me that effective management of your response to criticism is one of the key atrributes needed by the would-be-published. It can be startling to hear just how long those who did not quickly achieve publication kept persevering. The effective writer has to distinguish between valid criticism and negative vibes: in the long term, both can be motivating.

Questionnaire

Now turn to the questionnaire and think about how well you take rejection. Be honest. Does it spur you on or make you feel like giving up? Are you able to separate yourself from the writing, and look at it afresh, with a renewed determination to get into print? The answer you give does not have to be a summation of your lifetime's anti-rejection quota – just a snapshot right now (I would suggest that all answers should be reviewed after six months). Give yourself a mark out of ten for how good you are at handling rejection.

9

How well-read are you?

If you are trying to write a book, it may seem rather unhelpful to suggest that the best way of moving forward with your plan is to read books by other people. Reading takes time, and lack of time is the most common excuse for failing to get on with your own writing.

My reasoning is this. I have never met a good writer who is not also prolifically well-read. No matter the genre in which they write, it seems that a wide knowledge of literature is a precondition for being able to string words together yourself.

> "If you don't want to read, don't bother to write."
>
> Philip Pullman

> "Reading – I discovered – comes before writing. A society can exist – many do exist – without writing, but no society can exist without reading."
>
> Alberto Manguel (b1948), Argentinian writer

There are exceptions. Nancy Mitford (1904–73) claimed in her autobiography[1] that 'I have only read one book in my life, and that is *White Fang*'. Perhaps in her case, being surrounded by articulate people fuelled a desire to write. And there are occasionally 'celebrity' authors who claim to have been able to pen their story without first having read very much, but they are generally relying on ghost-writers to do the writing bit.

Please don't comfort yourself that your particular branch of literature has an easier entry point. Children's books are not for practice until you can write a full-length novel for adults:

---

1 *The Pursuit of Love.*

> "You must write for children in the same way as you do for adults, only better."
>
> Maksim Gorky (1868–1936), Russian novelist and playwright

Jacqueline Wilson, the best-selling children's author and current Children's Laureate, is one of the most well-read people I have ever met. I first came across her while attending a series of seminars she ran for readers in Kingston on the modern novel. We worked our way through the 20th century, a decade each time, and were hugely impressed by her ability to reference all sorts of books many of us had never heard of, let alone read.

There's a rich tradition of mocking the 'lady novelist' who writes romances (she is a subject of fun in Jane Austen's *Northanger Abbey* and made it on to Gilbert and Sullivan's 'little list'), but don't assume that if you decide to try this genre you will have an easier start. You are absolutely not absolved of reading widely; no lying on the sofa reciting and eating chocolate – unless you have done your homework first. The Romantic Novelists Association, which includes among its members many who write for the pink-covered Mills & Boon titles, is erudite, witty and extremely well-informed. On a visit to talk to their annual conference I met a former *Mastermind* winner, several very senior civil servants, JPs and numerous teachers, all well-read to a man or woman.

> "Each week I read at least one factual book – ecology or history, for example – plus a couple of novels, maybe a whodunit or a romantic comedy as well, plus anything else that catches my fancy. I also read old friends a lot, especially PG Wodehouse, Trollope, Diana Wynne Jones and Terry Pratchett. I don't take a daily newspaper and seldom read magazines, though."
>
> Jenny Haddon

> "Don't just read the type of book you're writing. I've written three memoirs on the trot, but I've read novels and heavy non-fiction along the way. A piece in the *New Yorker* can inspire me. Keep reading. Words fuel the fire."
>
> Andrew Collins

"Reading is vital for a writer because in the first instance, it's how you learn your craft. You often hear bestsellers say, 'I wrote the book I wanted to read.' They reason they knew that this gap in the market existed because they had read widely. My book group tells me I read differently because I'm a writer, but I deny this. When faced with something wonderful, I'm taken by the hand as much as any reader.

A hugely respected editor, who was also a writer (Diane Pearson), told me that when her authors came to her with writers' block, she'd tell them to go on a reading jag and read everything they could lay their hands on."

Katie Fforde

"I wrote my first novel because I wanted to read it."

Toni Morrison (b1931), US writer

Why is reading widely so important?

As an example of the art you seek to excel at yourself

"Good writers are generally, first and foremost, good readers; their instinct to explore what Dorothea Brande calls the 'magic' of writing comes because they have been convinced by the power of what other writers have done. They're also a certain kind of reader, not simply satisfied to accept what others have achieved on their behalf, but interested in understanding, pursuing, developing how it's done. What pushes them onward is a strong sense of inner motivation, and an effective capacity to organise and manage their impulses, instincts and artistic techniques to which they're willing to devote their lives."

Malcolm Bradbury (see bibliography)

"A great deal of research on writing instruction shows that learning the finer details of grammar has small effect on writing ability. Writers are far better off reading and writing, that is, learning to write by absorption, imitation, and practice, the way they learned to speak ... Although there's no single way writing should 'sound',

> reading with your eyes open to style allows you to see how other writers achieved an effective voice, and this is an essential step towards developing into a good writer yourself."
>
> Joe Glaser, *Understanding Style* (see bibliography)

So, in short, reading other people's work shows you how it is done – or as Richard Steele, essayist, playwright and politician (1672–1729) said:

> "Reading is to the mind what exercise is to the body."

To keep you up to date with what is being published

Most writers want to know who is hot and who is not. Sometimes this will be a source of frustration, particularly if you feel that someone less talented than you is getting published or enjoying a bigger marketing spend; but if you are going to communicate with agents and publishers about why your work is special, you need to know how to differentiate it from everything else. This is a very useful shorthand when communicating with publishers: to suggest that your work is a development of a particular writer, or a combination of two, will help them pitch your work. For example:

> "A cross between Nick Hornby and Ben Elton, but from the perspective of teenaged boy."

Be careful with your comparisons, though. Is it really possible, as I saw recently, for a book to: '… stand comparison with Scott Turow's *Presumed Innocent*, John Grisham's *The Firm* and Thomas Harris' *Red Dragon*'? The three are surely quite different.

If you decide to stand apart from your contemporaries, and not engage with writing you do not like, recognition may come if the ideas are strong enough – though perhaps not within your lifetime. An interesting example here is the reading habit of Iris Murdoch. The working library from her Oxford home was purchased by Kingston University in 2004 and a Centre for Iris Murdoch Studies has subsequently been established there. The books in her library provide a clue as to how she read. Sentences are underlined; exclamation marks pepper the margins, as do occasional notes; and in the end-pages of many of the books there are full notes on the content and records of her debates with philosophers. Dr Anne Rowe, Senior Lecturer in English and Murdoch specialist, commented:

"Iris Murdoch's personal library comprised an eclectic mix of books, mostly on philosophy, but also on theology, psychology, visual art and travel. She read the classics, Homer, Shakespeare, Austen, Dickens, Tolstoy, Dostoevsky and Proust, but she did not read contemporary fiction, a fact confirmed by her husband, John Bayley in his memoir *Iris*, written when she was stricken with Alzheimer's: 'She hardly ever read a contemporary novel ... she had no experience of what novels today were like.'

Iris Murdoch's dual role as both moral philosopher and novelist meant that her novels were intrinsically moral and, as such, fell out of fashion during the age of the post-modern, when moral content was regarded with suspicion. This, coupled with the sheer difficulty of her novels and the narrow, upper-class literary *milieu* in which they are set, rendered her books sometimes impenetrable, often unpalatable. But Murdoch resolutely refused to conform to current literary trends; she continued to forge her own way in blissful ignorance of what other contemporary writers were up to. Her insistence on the novel as a moral agent has reaped rewards now that the pendulum of literary criticism has swung in the opposite direction, and the moral function of literature has come back onto the critical agenda, thus making her unique position as moral philosopher and novelist more interesting than ever."

One final point about knowing what else is being published. If you do make it into print, you may find yourself being asked to give talks to groups of aspiring writers, and occasionally to present a prize. Having asked you to talk, you will probably find that what people want to hear about is *how* you did it, so that they can learn from what was evidently a successful approach. The more you mention the titles of your own books, the less likely people are to buy them. This is something I have observed at literary festivals up and down the country; the writer who talks about the genre they are active in, makes generous reference to other writers, and does not bang on obsessively about their own book, will sign and sell more copies at the end of the event. You have been warned.

"We had a celebrity along to launch the chain's Christmas book catalogue. All those whose books had been included had been asked. Maybe she had been badly briefed, but the usual thing is to talk about *all* the books being celebrated, not just her own in minute detail. I thought it was really selfish behaviour: if I had wanted to buy it beforehand, I certainly did not want to afterwards."

To refresh your ideas

"If you want to be a writer, you must do two things above all others: read a lot and write a lot. There's no way around these two things that I'm aware of, no shortcut ... Every book you pick up has its own lesson or lessons, and quite often the bad books have more to teach than the good ones ... You cannot hope to sweep someone else away by the force of your writing until it has been done to you ... So we read to experience the mediocre and the outright rotten; such experience helps us recognise those things when they begin to creep into our own work, and to steer clear of them. We also read in order to measure ourselves against the good and the great, to get a sense of all that can be done. And we read in order to experience different styles."

Stephen King

"I read a great deal. I couldn't bear not to. All the writers I know are very keen readers. As I'm always in the process of writing a book I read whatever I fancy – I don't find it interferes with my writing or influences it in any way. I think it's very important for all writers to read."

Jacqueline Wilson

"If I'm writing a sitcom I'll occasionally watch a sitcom during a break, like *Seinfeld*, something impeccably good, to have some-thing unattainable to aim for!"

Andrew Collins

"I don't think it's possible to be a good writer if you don't read! And not just the classics, either – read contemporary stuff, especially the genre you are writing in. I also love to read biographies of other writers. If you think that, as a woman, it is difficult to find time to write, you should read the letters of Harriet Beecher Stowe."

Trisha Ashley

Reading widely, and across genres, introduces you to new ways of writing about things: new adjectives, new combinations and new stimuli.

To put you in touch with great minds
Through reading, it is possible to absorb fine thoughts, as if by osmosis.

"I love to lose myself in other men's minds. When I am not walking, I am reading; I cannot sit and think. Books think for me."

Charles Lamb (1775–1834), essayist

"The reading of all good books is like a conversation with the finest men of past centuries."

Rene Descartes (1596–1650), French philosopher

But while we should enjoy finer minds than ours, don't get dispirited. Great literature is usually not the writer's first book.

To extend you
CS Lewis said that we write in order to know that we are not alone. Reading gives us new insights into things we did not formerly understand. Writing is an exercise in empathy; we can only understand other people by thinking ourselves into their shoes. Reading what others have written helps us do that.

"Reading, to me, is simply the expansion of one's mind to include some people whom you just didn't get to meet before."

Ntozake Shange (b1948), US poet and novelist

"Read in order to live."

Gustave Flaubert (1821–80), French novelist

"I think it's essential to read, and not just books (fiction and non-fiction) but newspapers, magazines, and to watch TV, listen to radio and go the cinema. Opening yourself up to a variety of influences is a healthy part of the writing process as it enables you to sample different ways in which information is delivered and be aware of new ideas."

Adam Powley

That's not to say you have to like everything you read ... but without having tried, how can you have an opinion?

"I have tried lately to read Shakespeare, and found it so intolerably dull that it nauseated me."

Charles Darwin (1809–1992), British naturalist

Reading in practice: how to go about it

Don't just read in the genre you like. Reading – or observing what is being read – may give you new ideas for new markets, new formats:

"You have to read as widely as you can – not just books you like and feel comfortable with, but books you dislike, books that are difficult or frustrating to read, books that are unsettling. Read old books as well as new books, experimental books as well as traditional ones, biographies and non-fiction as well as novels, books in translation as well as books in English. The more you read, the better you'll write."

Kate Grenville (see bibliography)

So go ahead and enjoy *The Spectator* and *The Beano*; *The Daily Telegraph* and *The Mirror*. Look at how arguments are constructed, consider sentence lengths, the level of vocabulary. Cut out your favourites and stick them on a board in your writing room.

As you progress, look at particularly fine passages and take them apart; see what you can learn from them. Have an ongoing competition for your favourite sentence or phrase. Mine is from Jane Austen:

> "... her love of dirt gave way to an inclination for finery ..."
>
> (from *Northanger Abbey*)

I love the way the monosyllables give way to polysyllables, matching the sense of the phrase.

Examine sentence length and see how this is varied according to the stage in the story, the character or the position in the paragraph. It's important to learn to read as a writer; reading critically to work out why things do or don't work can make bad books tolerable. And then come back and study the great.

> "Reading is important for a writer, but re-reading is also vital. To me, Jane Austen is like a blood transfusion. There is no way that you can return to writing after reading her and remain untouched. The superb quality of her English pushes you away from drabness."
>
> Brian Cathcart

Look out for new words, of any kind, to inspire you. At home we have a regular game over meals to find your favourite word. A writer friend had parents who each week would write on a board in the kitchen the 'word of the week', which everyone had to use as often as possible. Read aloud to children; there is nothing better for creating an articulate person. Try to listen to articulate people on the radio or television. I prefer the former medium as it throws greater emphasis on the vocabulary being used. We regularly listen to Radio 4's *The News Quiz* twice, to ensure we catch everything!

When to read

When you should do all this reading is a little harder to specify. Many writers I have spoken to read before they start to write each morning, so as to warm their brain up. Once they have started to write they keep away from other people's work so as to avoid 'infecting' their own style:

> "The essence of serious writing is that it's not a struggle to repeat what others have done, but a struggle not to."
>
> Malcolm Bradbury

This can seem a terrible trial when you are eager to find displacement activity, but try hard to put off what Brande refers to as the 'debauches of book buying', until you have finished writing yourself. Alternatively, pile books up next to your bed as a form of deferred gratification; think of them as the swim you long for on a hot day and sit beside the pool preparing for it, giving you an extra incentive to finish. I can remember longing to read romantic fiction stories in my mother's *Woman and Home* magazines while I was preparing for my 'O' levels, and rationing myself to one a day. Oddly, once I had finished the exams and could read what I liked, they did not seem so tempting.

> "If you are writing a manuscript so long that the prospect of not reading at all until you have finished is too intolerable, be sure to choose books which are as unlike your own work as possible: read technical books, history, or, best of all, books in other languages."
>
> Dorothea Brande

> "I think reading is a worse vice for a writer than alcohol or drugs, and equally addictive. A lot of fiction writers stick to reading non-fiction. If you stop reading you get desperate and start reading adverts and computer instruction manuals. It makes you write stories because you're deprived of reading them."
>
> Nicholas Allan

> "I used to 'buy all the albums' and read everything by a particular author in a brief, intense period of time – I've done this with Peter Carey, Jane Austen, Somerset Maugham, Graham Greene and Gabriel Garcia Marquez. And I suppose – apart from Austen – most of those authors are significant influences on my writing (hence my wariness of reading while I'm writing myself)."
>
> Sunil Badami

"The only thing I regret about taking up writing is that I read much, much less. It's not because I want to; it's because of the time. I have a full-time job and write several books a year – and there's no time to read as much as I used to. I do think it's the most important thing you can do, except for writing, and I try to make time for it, because I miss it a lot."

Julie Cohen

How to cheat – sounding 'well read' without the effort of reading

"There are two motives for reading a book: one, that you enjoy it, the other is that you can boast about it."

Bertrand Russell (1872–1970), philosopher

- Learn to skim-read, or read enough of a book to be able to bullshit with confidence. This is particularly easy to do with non-fiction, and I confess that I have talked about both *No Logo* and *Emotional Intelligence* without reading the whole of either. The introduction, a few chapters, a detailed look at the contents list and the conclusion is usually enough.

"The art of reading is to skip judiciously."

Philip Hamerton (1834–94), art critic

"He has only half learned the art of reading who has not added to it the even more refined accomplishments of skipping and skimming."

Arthur Balfour (1848–1930), Prime Minister

- Visit your local bookshop or library and read book blurbs (the words on the back cover of a paperback or the flaps of a hardcover jacket).
- Read book reviews in the press. Each newspaper has book reviews that sum up and give you a flavour of what is inside. The amount the book is talked about in the review depends on the point of view of the reviewer and how much their interests overlap with the author's. Reviews can be variously enlightening.

Sometimes one senses that the reviewer has used the book's title to provide a vehicle for writing a piece they had in mind in any case, in which case the reader gets a point of view as well as a book title to refer to in conversation:

"I was so long writing my review that I never got around to reading the book."

Groucho Marx (1895–1977), comedian

- Look on the bookshelves of those you respect and see which books are displayed, in which combinations. It was on this basis that I decided to read VS Naipaul.
- Carry a book at all times. Even the busiest life can accommodate reading. Just carrying a book at all times can provide opportunities because:

"You just never know when you'll want an escape hatch."

Stephen King

"I read on trains and buses, even walking along the street sometimes. It's a wonder I don't hurt myself, but I have a technique of regular glancing up to survey an area of about 20 feet immediately ahead for possible hazards and walking quite slowly. Pavements are hazardous, and my favourite is to walk on a path around the part where I live near Greenwich Park, which has a path all the way round the perimeter, just inside the wall. I pretend I am a monk in a cloister."

Sheila Cornelius

How to be well-read *quickly*

This interesting idea was explored recently on the radio programme *A Good Read*, with Professor Lisa Jardine recommending five books that would give those listening to you an instant sense that you knew about books. She chose:

- A classic (probably 19th century, perhaps George Eliot's *Middlemarch* or a novel by Jane Austen or Charles Dickens).

- A key book of thought or philosophy (JP Sartre's *Being and Nothingness*).

- A name to drop (e.g. a writer in translation, little known, but with a growing reputation – perhaps Rabindranath Tagore, the brahmin poet and thinker).

- A modern novel (e.g. Zadie Smith's *White Teeth*, Gillian Slovo's *The Ice Age*, or *Enduring Love* by Ian McEwan).

- A book of influential style (such as Virginia Woolf's *To the Lighthouse* or *St John's Gospel* [2]).

Alternatively, there are compendia of books with summaries so you can name-drop or sound familiar with plots you need to memorise. And then of course there are books of literary criticism. Stephen Fry confessed to writing an undergraduate essay about *Middlemarch* solely from reading the commentaries, as he thought it a book of 'ridiculous' length.

Questionnaire

So, how well-read are you? Are you the kind of person who can't stop reading, even bus tickets or free newspapers over other people's shoulders? What about your reading in the past? Would you qualify on the scale of Jacqueline Wilson or Professor Jardine's abbreviated course? It was the universal opinion of all the writers I consulted that if you don't have time to read, you are not equipped to write. Have you read enough to take yourself seriously as a writer?

Now give yourself a mark out of ten (bearing in mind that you can always improve your score in the meantime), and note the result on the questionnaire.

2 Preferably the Revised Standard Version (RSV), 1946.

10

How much do you know about the publishing industry?

I can imagine that you may feel tempted to skip this chapter. If you want to write a book, surely it's up to the publishing industry to deal with what you produce, in the same way that you don't need to know about banking in order to accept financial services from a branch of Barclays.

Resist the temptation. If you understand how the industry works, you really do stand a better chance of getting into print.

Who does what?

Literary agents

Literary agents act for authors. They try to match each author they represent with the most appropriate publishing house. To do this, they use their previous experience of the industry, based on the house's past track-record; the personality, interests and attitude to risk of the commissioning editor they are approaching; and the amount of money on offer. Agents are also keen to help a writer develop their career, and will be thinking not just about the book in the writer's head at the moment, but also about the direction this will take them in future. They are paid on a percentage of the author's earnings (usually 15% of receipts), so it is in their interests not just to secure the highest advance[1] (which after all may not be fully repaid through sales) but also to ensure a slice of attention and marketing budget from the publishing house they opt for.

Agents receive a huge number of manuscripts ever day – Carole Blake of Blake-Friedmann told me recently that she gets between

30 and 50 every day, and more on a Friday. And because they sift through the list before passing what they like on to publishers, you definitely stand a better chance of being taken seriously by a publishing house if your manuscript reaches them endorsed by an agent, than if it is accompanied by a letter on your own headed paper. There are occasions on which unsolicited manuscripts submitted directly to publishers by individual authors (these comprise what is unengagingly termed the 'slush pile') end up being selected for stardom – Mary Stewart was an example – but these are remarkable precisely because they are rare. It is difficult to get non-fiction agented, and most authors in this category contact publishers direct. If you have a choice of agents, and all seem similarly qualified in a professional sense, go for someone you get along with; sharing the revenue you created by writing, with someone who irks you, can only get more difficult.

It is worth pointing out that of late, a new strand has emerged in the publishing chain – that of literary consultant. Literary consultancies are growing fast. They offer a paid-for service and will review a manuscript, give frank advice on whether it is publishable, and then advise on how to submit an idea to an agent.

In general, agents are well-informed, passionate about books (many editors become agents in order to have more time to work with writers – something that gets squeezed out of the increasingly bureaucratic life of the publisher), fond of personal publicity and not immune to vanity (so observing who they have looked after and with what success will always go down well). Remember, though, that they earn their money from an author's efforts. While their motivation in promoting good writing to a captivated public is not in doubt, they have to make money as they do so – or they

---

1 An advance is the payment made to an author on commission. An amount is agreed and it is usually paid so much on signature, so much on delivery and acceptance, and so much on publication (usually one-third in each case, but this is open to negotiation). The author does not start earning royalties (or an agreed commission on each title sold) until the amount of the advance has been earned (or 'earned out', in publishing speak). Many books never earn their advance, making the commissioning of a second title from the same author a questionable business decision.

will not be around for the next lot of ideas. It's reckoned these days that it's harder to get taken on by an agent than by a publisher.

Publishers

Publishers produce books (and increasingly a range of other products such as CDs, websites and related merchandise, e.g. branded toys and stationery). Each house will have a range of different imprints,[2] under which related titles will come out. For example, the Penguin children's list is published under the imprint of Puffin, and Ebury is an imprint of Random House. Many imprints were previously independent companies; if you want to know who publishes a particular imprint, the umbrella organisation is listed on a page near the front of the book.

Most publishers are looking for titles that will fit within their existing stable – it's easier and more cost-effective to market, and hence to sell, several titles at the same time. Publishers sell their wares to booksellers in the hope that they will stock them, or sell them direct to the end user.

The commissioning editor is on the lookout for good ideas which either fit the list[3] or which would take it in an interesting new direction. This is primarily an ideas-based, outward-looking job. **The copy editor** is the person who goes through a manuscript looking out for editorial consistency and whether or not you are using clear English. It's important to understand these two very different roles, and be clear about which type of editor you are speaking to.

There is routine confusion between the meaning of 'marketing' and 'sales' in the wider world, but within publishing houses the roles are different. Marketing is involved in deciding where the consumer is, and how best to target messages to them. **Marketing staff** are on the lookout for as many – and as low-cost as possible – avenues to reach the end user. **Sales staff** estimate how many copies will be sold and where. Their approval in the meeting that decides whether or not to publish is absolutely crucial; a carefully presented information pack from the commissioning editor about

2 A grouping of similar titles under a particular trademark.

3 'The list' is the publisher's catalogue of existing and planned titles. 'Not fitting the list' is the most common reason for rejecting an author's new idea for a book.

an author who can write beautifully can be rejected if the sales staff do not believe enough copies can sell. Of course, decisions are often made on a long-term basis – will this author one day win the Booker prize; can they be built into a brand that will become popular; do we need a writer of romantic fiction who is under 30 to have more appeal with younger readers, and is this the writer we should invest in?

Once the final manuscript has been agreed, **production staff** are responsible for getting the book out on time in an acceptable format. They will have to weigh up cost and accessibility; thus, printing in China may save money, but it may be a false economy if the much more complicated liaison arrangements and additional time needed for importing delay publication. **Rights staff** sell the right to other publishing houses to produce special editions for different territories, and translation rights into different languages; thus the UK edition of a book may look different from that produced for the French market. Sometimes even for other English-language markets the words are changed to match local spelling (e.g. analyse/analyze) but for other markets it may be concluded that this is a needless expense (e.g. for the majority of academic and business titles).

In general, publishers come from a limited gene pool. While there have been important initiatives to widen the range of those employed in the industry, it remains largely white, middle-class and well-spoken. There are many more Carolines than Kylies, many more arts than science graduates. Publishers often have to be educated about markets of which they have no understanding, or for which they feel a genuine distaste (Jordan's autobiography was turned down by most agents and yet went on to be a major seller). Publishers also tend to agree with each other most of the time, and are often happiest copying what other publishers have already produced rather than producing something new or for which there is popular – but so far undemonstrated – demand (most people know that *Harry Potter* was turned down by many publishers). It follows that if your idea is for a market or a product with which they are unlikely to be familiar, you are best served explaining what the market is, how to reach it, what else proves it (other synergistic developments in society that reveal a trend), and why they should bother. The 'why they should bother' is profit, which you should always bear in mind as the justification for publishing: it is not simply a literary service to society.

> "As repressed sadists are supposed to become policemen or butchers, so those with an irrational fear of life become publishers."
>
> Cyril Connolly (1903–74), British writer and journalist

> "I usually feel guilty, because I am usually behind where I ought to be. I think that they would be wise to keep in closer contact with me – that way they would have more chance to get me to do what they want. I have always had a bit of a battle with editors because I hate them thinking they know more about grammar than me – and I guess this has become reinforced as I've got older and they've got younger. I think all my publishing contacts bar two have been women – and they have all been very charming and pleasant, even if I have not been."
>
> Professor Gwyneth Pitt

> "I think it helps to see the book trade as more and more resembling the film industry. The cult of the author is a little bit misleading these days. No one really knows or cares who wrote the script of the latest blockbuster movie. The writer is pretty low on that food chain, and he has to work with producers and stars to get a product out. If Star X won't do horse riding, then they have to rewrite. If Director Y thinks a scene is necessary then it has to be written. Everyone puts an oar in. The writer has to collaborate. This may sound like a massive compromise, but writers in the film business often say that if you are compliant on one little thing (some pesky note from a executive producer, for example) the big things, the things that matter to you in the project, will get past.
>
> Of course, this might sound a bit like collaborating with the Nazis. On the other hand, talking through things with other people with different viewpoints and creativity of their own can strengthen and inform what you are doing. I think you can be too proud sometimes. But remember, if they did not have us they would have nothing to sell."
>
> Harriet Smart

"The worst thing about trying to get a novel published is the waiting. It just goes on and on. And then all of a sudden there is frantic interest in something you finished ages ago, and you can hardly remember because you are so into the next book. I am normally quite confident, but publishers and agents terrorise me – I am too scared to ring them in case they tell me the thing I most don't want to hear."

Novelist

"I have written several books that are award winners, although none has been an outright bestseller. None of my books has lost money for its publisher. Yet when I go to meetings with publishers to discuss what I might write next, I find they are far keener to talk about themselves – and their own book ideas – than my work. They have never read what I sent in beforehand, and they make judgements too quickly, without enough thought. They are self-obsessed and have a terrible tendency to name-drop."

Non-fiction author

"I remember Diana Athill talking about the four or five book apprenticeship, where a publisher would let a writer develop their own voice before hitting paydirt on the fifth book, and reaping some return from the backlist as well. However, now it seems that every first book – being semi-autobiographical and thus written for the writer's entire life – is so big and so stuffed with so much (*à la White Teeth* or *Brick Lane* or *God of Small Things*) that it'll always be naturally difficult to follow that up with something different. Imagine if Somerset Maugham had stopped being published after the now-forgotten follow-up to *Liza of Lambeth*? Or Graham Greene after *The Name of Action* or *Rumour at Nightfall*? There's a lot of pressure, especially on young, unproven writers, to try and say everything they can say, because they may not get another chance."

Sunil Badami

"Publishers are just wonderful at mucking their authors around. They seem to have slight understanding of what being creative and productive really takes. A little mutual respect would not go amiss – without us they would have nothing to sell."

Fiction author

Booksellers

Booksellers today hold the balance of power. They can demand to buy books at a huge discount on the full retail price, and there is often extra discount on offer for 'additional promotion' within their stores (a display at the front of the shop, putting a title in the window and running a special discount are all counted as 'extra' these days). The emphasis on '3 for 2' and in-store discounts has meant that the range of titles on which publishers can offer these hugely advanced discounts (usually called 'terms') is reduced, and the same titles tend to be on offer in every different chain store. This means that the high-selling authors are richer than ever before, but that those in the middle (the 'mid list') are seeing their incomes decline dramatically. And of course there is a very real wariness on the part of publishers to take risks; to take a punt on titles that might do well if they catch the public imagination, but might not – particularly unlikely if the book trade is not willing to stock them.

Due to an anachronistic but established practice within the trade, booksellers also lack financial responsibility for the stock they order, in that what has not sold within a short window of time (routinely three weeks for a new work of fiction by an unknown author) can be sent back to the publisher for a refund. This practice was originally established on the grounds that it encouraged booksellers to take a wide variety of stock, but has persisted to the extent that it surely undermines booksellers' commitment to what they have chosen, and the necessity of stocking with care.

Bookshop managers vary in the amount of latitude they have to choose what is on the shelves in their store. Large chains have a limited number of 'A' list titles to choose between and they are largely told how many of each to stock. Other titles, they can order. Subject **buyers** have responsibility for individual sections of the shop: publishers' reps show new titles to them and, depending on the store's policy, they can decide to stock them or not. Sometimes corporate policy means that whatever the local knowledge of the bookseller, standard stocking policies are adhered to:

"I worked at the bookshop within a major concert venue. We had people who were really serious about music coming in ready to pay large amounts of cash for hard-backed editions of the books they wanted. But instead of attracting them in with our well-stocked and varied window display, we had to put multiple copies of the crime fiction that had been agreed nationally. I am convinced this substantially diminished passing trade."

Bookseller

"I hate shopping. My husband does not want me to look like everyone else. I drive past a 'boutique' shop I like in Wimbledon village twice a day, and if there is something in the window I fancy when I go past in the morning, I leave early for my return trip in the afternoon and try it on. They change the window often enough to give me something new to look at."

Rich and very upwardly mobile mother, overheard
at a focus group on Boden clothes recently

Both publishers and booksellers tend to job-hop with a frequency that alarms authors. But while publishers tend to stay in the business, moving from house to house and sometimes taking their authors with them, booksellers go on to other retail outlets.

In general, the role of the bookseller has changed dramatically in recent years. Once largely ignored by publishers, who would give them what they had decided to sell, today the buying power of booksellers is enormous and they can – and do – dictate the survival of authors. Their buying procedures, in some cases ill-thought-through, can dictate what is available to the reading public. The application of buying and marketing practices that are standard within retailing as a whole to bookselling (e.g. charging for seeing reps or putting stuff in the window) has caused huge resentment within the world of publishing.

Another important character within this world is the **independent bookseller,** who takes a stand against the monochromatic uniformity of large chain stores. The independent bookseller eschews offering the public a discount in favour of stocking a wide range of titles, and likes to be seen as providing the discerning reader with a service: enthusiastic recommendation; a passion for books;

the chance to meet like-minded souls. It should be noted however that independent booksellers rely more than other retailers on customer loyalty; it follows that they look for a relationship with their local authors rather than a one-way flow of admiration and support.

"We are always delighted when one of our customers tells us they are having a book published and we offer enthusiastic support. We'll happily give opinions on jackets, help with research, hold local launch parties, and, when the book is right for our market, we'll feature piles of signed copies. These are good two-way relationships, which benefit everyone.

Our hearts sink, however, when we're approached by an author whom we've never seen before, who proudly announces that they're having a book published and that they're a local author. We always wonder where they've been buying their books from. Writers who don't shop in their local bookshop shouldn't expect that same bookshop to be delighted at their appearance with offers to sign copies. Selling books is hard work. It takes effort to promote and sell titles well. Sometimes it takes monetary support too, in the form of discounts. We will always work hard to support writers we know, and importantly who make an effort to get to know us. We don't expect to be asked to devote our energies to supporting writers who buy their books from Waterstone's or Amazon.

Sometimes we are contacted by authors who are not local to us, such as Deborah Lawrenson, who wrote to us following an article in *The Bookseller*. Her novel *The Art of Falling* had been self-published and had gained the enthusiastic support of booksellers in her local Ottaker's. Many copies were sold and the book came to the attention of Arrow who offered her a contract for a mass market edition. Her letter to us struck just the right note – polite, funny and importantly not pushy. We looked up her book, like it and promoted it enough to sell around 100 copies in paperback."

Hazel Broadfoot, The Bookshop, Dulwich Village

What do all sectors of the book world want from authors?

Here's a revolutionary thought. Publishing houses, agents and booksellers are much more interested in how your potential new title fits with the list they already market/the customers they already have access to, than how much you want to write a book. And so, while you are pouring your soul out into your writing and regarding yourself, your talent and your motivation as of fundamental importance, you may get a better response from publishers if you look at yourself from *their* point of view. Adapting the famous JFK statement from his inaugural speech, think not what they can do for you, but what you can do for them.

> "When you can present your own ideas clearly, specifically, visually, and most important, contextually – in the context of a deep understanding of their paradigms and concerns – you significantly increase the credibility of your ideas."
>
> Stephen R Covey (see bibliography)

The starting qualification for any potential supplier – and that's what authors are to publishers – is that they can deliver the goods to an agreed quality by a certain date. Your ability to do this will be the baseline for any future relationship with a publisher. They are not interested in how long you have wanted to write for; only in that if they sign you up, you will be able to deliver and sustain production of items of similar quality, in the future.

> "I will never forget that without publishers I wouldn't have achieved my dream. They want to get the best possible book out of you and to sell as many copies as possible. As long as you both realise that you are BOTH working to the same end, life's a breeze. A brilliant editor is a must, and I've had very wonderful editors, but they also have to be able to work with the marketing/publicity departments, and sometimes that's trickier to achieve. Your editor has to sell your work to the rest of the company, and so they need more than editing skills."
>
> Nicola Morgan

How to approach publishers and agents

Most publishers specialise. They find that the best way of approaching a market is to have a consistent profile, so that booksellers come to trust what they are offering, and a reputation for reliability can be established. So if they say they do not commission romantic fiction, do not assume that by offering it you are helpfully extending their range for them. On the other hand, referring to a title they have had considerable success with, and showing that you understand their list, may well get a relationship off to a good start.

Your starting point should be a copy of the *Writers' & Artists' Yearbook*, which tells you who takes on what kind of book (publishers and agents) and how they like to be approached. The yearbook is awash with this kind of information; it says what format they like to receive information in and how to go about approaching them. Take this seriously. An invitation to send three chapters is just that, not 'as close to three chapters as you can get'.

When approaching agents and publishers, remember that they are people who care about words, so don't mis-spell their names or invite them to 'peruse' your manuscript (a word they all seem to hate; the book equivalent of mis-spelling 'liaise' on your CV[4]).

Get the firm's name right. Mr Hamish Hamilton is no longer running the eponymous firm he founded, it's now part of Penguin. Letters addressed to the agent 'Mr Curtis Brown' are similarly unlikely to impress. There was a Mr Curtis Brown – the founder Albert, then his son Spencer – but both have long since passed on, so letters that begin 'Dear Mr Curtis' or 'Dear Mr Brown', or even worse, 'Dear Sir or Madam', are immediately identified to be from people who have done no research into the firm. If anything about a manuscript makes it less than straightforward to read, it won't be read; a good mantra is to imagine that all recipients are short-sighted and in a hurry. Make sure the pages are clean, error-free, printed out in double-spaced format and in a typeface that is easy to read. If your work is dog-eared, the message is clear: the manuscript has been rejected before.

---

4 When those recruiting get too many responses, a commonly used technique for eliminating people is to cut out all those who mis-spell 'liaise'. A very common trap.

Your handling of grammar and parts of speech can be unorthadox, provided that it is consistent. For example, Livi Michael's *All the Dark Air* contains large amounts of conversation, but none of it is wrapped in speech marks. She did this to ensure that the whole book felt colloquial, to avoid any jarring difference between conversation and narrative; but the result is that the book has a calm, almost serene, feeling – a contrast with the depressing spiral of events chronicled. Crucially, the manuscript she submitted was entirely consistent.

You may be asked to submit a synopsis. This is a taster for the book as a whole; a tempter. Publishers and agents seldom need a chapter-by-chapter outline of who does what. What they need to know is what kind of book is it – uplifting, romantic, practical, money- or time-saving? What immediate benefits will the reader derive from it? A successful synopsis is best thought of as a book blurb, enticing the reader to want to know more.

How new authors get taken on

What follows is a generalisation; the names and formats will vary from house[5] to house, but the theory is similar. Please don't assume that if you are planning to write an academic text or a book of poetry, this advice does not apply to you – it is relevant *whatever* kind of publication you want to produce.

Most houses have commissioning editors who are on the lookout for new authors/potential talent. Sometimes they go out to find it; at other times they look for what comes through their door, either in the form of unsolicited manuscripts or from agents. At the same time, they are trying to spot people who can write for a particular project they have in mind.

"I had been thinking of producing a Bridget Jones diary for teenagers, and was on the lookout for a writer who could handle this. I spotted a piece written by Louise Rennison in the *Evening Standard* and thought she had just the right blend of vitality and

5 Publishing speak for organisation or company.

humour – humour that made me laugh out loud. I approached her to ask if she would like to write for us. *Angus, Thongs and Full-frontal Snogging* was the result, and we went on to publish several more highly successful diary novels about Georgia with her."

Brenda Gardner, Piccadilly Press

Once an author has made a positive impression on a commissioning editor, the editor must then convince his or her colleagues that this is a project worth investing in. Almost all publishing houses have a formal meeting, at regular intervals, at which publishing projects are outlined and decisions made on whether they should be taken any further. At this meeting it is the commissioning (or sponsoring) editor who presents the possible title to a collection of other people within the firm, who must be convinced of its merits before the project can go any further. These will include representation from sales (who will estimate how many books can be sold based on past experience of the market), marketing (who will decide how targetable the customer is, and through what means), publicity (how promoteable is the author?), production (what kind of product are we talking about, and how many pages, so we can get the price right?), distribution (what kind of sales outlets will it sell through?) and rights (who else might like to buy rights from us – i.e. the right to translate or produce in a different version, e.g. a branded product bearing a supermarket name, or a special-edition version for a corporate gift?).

Around a third of the publishing ideas presented will be taken further, and the editor has little time in which to make the pitch. If the presentation of one title takes longer, other presentations will have to be squeezed as the meeting invariably has an important, and pre-arranged, stopping time (like lunch).

Commissioning editors will prepare for the meeting by putting together a proposal for publication, but it will help your chances of getting published enormously if you give them interesting and helpful statistics about you and the project you have in mind. For example:

Where is the market for your book?
Can you quantify it, outline it, give a snapshot of what kind of person might buy it? The more specific you can be, the higher your

chances of being taken on, so the readership of a particular magazine that is relevant to a book you want to write is useful information.

My most recent book was a book on parenting teenagers, co-written with educator and trainer Gill Hines. There are not many books on this subject (publishers having up to now assumed that people only want books on having a baby and raising toddlers), so as part of making the pitch for our title we mentioned:

- The number of parents and teenagers in this country and elsewhere
- The growing popularity of television programmes on parenting
- The demand for modern-day information on morality and values (the rise of the Alpha Course, sales of popular philosophy titles by AC Grayling, the huge rise in philosophy as a popular study at university and in evening classes)

What is interesting about you?

Imagine you had ten seconds to engage someone's interest at a party. You would presumably start with something interesting rather than a chronological list of your achievements, public examination successes, and hobbies. Remember that agents and publishing houses are receiving thousands of submissions; what can you say about yourself that will make you stand out? This does not have to be anything earth-shattering, just something that makes you memorable.

> "John Harding was born in a small Fenland village in the island of Ely in 1951. After local village and grammar schools, he read English at St Catherine's College, Oxford, where he once sat next to Martin Amis during a lecture."
>
> From the short author blurb, John Harding, *What We Did on Our Holiday*

Having read this in a bookshop I deduced that the writer was very clever; something of an outsider; a long-time professional writer who would produce something worth reading; and, crucially, someone who would not take himself too seriously. The book was very enjoyable.

What is your book called?

Many authors make the mistake of assuming that the title of their book can be thought of later. Not so: it matters hugely. Publishing houses and agents want something that will attract immediate attention; a title that will titillate. Graham Norton's choice of a title for his first one-man show demonstrated an admirable pragmatism:

> "Then, one day, in between the spuds in the spunk, a title for my show came to me. It would be called 'Mother Teresa of Calcutta's Grand Farewell Tour'. I still had no idea what was going to be in the show, but I knew that I would buy a ticket to a show with that title."[6]

> "My first book was about life as an Army wife, a world that most people know very little about, but which can be fascinating – all those uniforms and odd practices! I had the bright idea of calling my book 'Hors de Combat' which is a military term and I thought a rather splendid pun (hors=whore). But it did imply you needed French, and not everyone knew the term. My publishers quite rightly suggested we called it *Army Wives*, as this said exactly what it did on the label! I like to think that *Stepford Wives* and *Footballers' Wives* were following the successful formula I established!"
>
> Catherine Jones

> "It's either good or not, and you can usually tell from the title."
>
> Kate Rowland, Creative Director of New Writing, BBC

What success have you had in the past?

See chapter 2 for advice on writing in other formats.

What is your book like?

Categorise and name successes. Be specific; your work can't be like that of Thomas Hardy and John Grisham at the same time. What kind of book is it – and where would it sit in a bookshop? If publishers can't think how to categorise it, or booksellers where they would put it, the easiest option for both will be to say no to the whole project.

---

6 From *So Me*, the autobiography of Graham Norton, Hodder and Stoughton, 2004.

Is it part of a growing area or one that is contracting? It pays all would-be authors to wander round bookshops and note which sections of the shop are expanding and which are being cut back. Are there any new subject headings which seem to attract a lot of traffic? For example, most shops now seem to have a 'Creative Writing' section as well as a 'Parenting' one. A few years ago these were part of 'Reference' and 'Childcare', so they bear witness to the expanding number of such titles required by customers.

If a bookshop has a coffee shop, look at the shelf where people put books they have looked at but do not want to buy. What can you learn from the rejects? This can be just as revealing as looking at lists of what is selling well. In libraries, the 'just returned' shelves work in a different way – it is here that regular visitors look to see what has just come back in, and these books get borrowed most – again, ideal market research for a writer.

If what you want to write is a completely new venture, and nothing like it has appeared before (perhaps the first account of the gladiatorial arena from the lion's point of view), then it is particularly important to explain why this is interesting, and who you think will buy it. No competition could mean an open market ripe for sales, but it could also mean that there is no market.

Who else likes your work?

Look on the back cover of any book jacket and you will see endorsements from appropriate people. Sometimes these come from reviews; more often they are sought by the publisher or author before publication. Do you know anyone whose endorsement might help? The person does not have to be famous, just relevant – so if you are writing a children's book, the recommendation of a child of the right age would be an advantage, or a class teacher who has enjoyed reading it to their pupils. Not all first-time authors are so well-connected, but it can help to get you get noticed. Look through your address book; if you really put your mind to it you probably know more people who could provide a recommendation than you think.

Be reassuring

Taking a punt on a new writer is a risk: you need to reassure your agent and publisher that it is one worth taking. So reassuring them with answers to other questions raised in this book will help. For example, they will want to know how well-established is your writing habit – but they will be more reassured by the information that you have part-time income to support your writing than that you have already given up your day job and are devoting yourself to writing the manuscript they have in front of them. They will be keen to know that you are proactive and imaginative – but are more likely to be convinced of these qualities if you give them examples of what has worked for you. For example:

> "I suggested to a local bookseller that I read during one of the 'open mike' sessions they offer within their store and got the local paper along to cover the occasion."

This will be better received than:

> "My book appeals to the general reader and should sell well through my local bookshop."

How marketing-savvy are you?

The most commonly used word in marketing meetings is 'promote-able' and it matters enormously. Gone are the days when authors could deliver their manuscript and retire to West Wittering to count the royalties. These days, authors are expected to take part in the marketing as well. At publication time they will be expected to appear on the radio and television (without giving their publicity person a hard time if nothing is set up), to travel to and from London on consecutive days (without insisting that the two appointments be on the same day), and to write articles for publication that support the book (but probably do not attract an additional fee). And however famous the writer, they will still be needed to take part in this process. So the more you can demonstrate that you understand the power of publicity and are not media-shy, the better your chance of securing a publishing deal.

"My advice is to take a keen interest in all aspects of the selling process. It's a way of life, and it would be snooty to opt out of it. Also, it's your book at the end of the day, with your name on."

Andrew Collins

What to do with all this information

Assemble all this information onto a few sheets of A4 and lay it out in a manner that is interesting. Do not justify the text (leaving the right-hand margin ragged makes it easier to engage with the words immediately; justified text has a very 'closed look'), and add lots of sub-headings to make it as easy to skim-read as possible. Include illustrations where relevant, and give all photographs an interesting caption. (An important caveat: while what you supply will be invaluable in helping those whom you wish to publish you to make that decision, this kind of preparation and research cannot take the place of being able to write.)

Other options for getting published

"I feel very distant from publishers. I think I've improved my writing over the last 5–6 years, and I do feel bitter that there's no mainstream outlet for my work. Sometimes this makes me angry, but I try to focus on getting my work out (slowly) in a more localised area, and making it, as far as I can, the best that I can. I do however think that the UK market is very conservative and limited in what it allows in. That may of course just be my own failure speaking. I'm only human, darn it!"

Anne Brooke

Vanity publishing is probably the best-known alternative. You provide your manuscript and pay up front for it to be processed; the 'publisher' will put varying amounts of effort into preparing your work for publication. Printed copies are delivered to you, and it is up to you what you do with them – store them under your bed or try to sell them.

Self-publishing is an increasingly popular option, and there are several firms offering authors the chance to have their manuscript published and to opt into whatever services of a traditional publisher they decide are most relevant. For example, you could decide that you want assistance with editorial presentation and manuscript organisation, provide the image to go on the front of the jacket yourself, and ask for a very small print run to circulate just to your immediate family. Alternatively you might decide that you want help with persuading wholesalers to stock the title, and advice on the marketing, but are confident that the editorial side of things can be handled by you.

Summary

For those of you who have made it to the end, I realise that this chapter will probably have burdened you with a lot of detail you did not think you needed to know. After all, your aim is to write a book, not find a job in publishing or book retailing. If you still feel like this, can you remarket the concept to yourself as 'exploring your craft' or 'deepening your understanding of your profession'? After all, as the Chinese proverb goes:

"If you want to catch a fish you have got to think like a fish."

Questionnaire

Now look at the questionnaire at the end of this book. Think carefully about how much you know about the world of books, and how much this will either help or hinder you in your desire to be published. Then give yourself a mark out of ten.

In the long run, this is something you can build on as you write and encourage family and friends to do the same. Give yourself six months, look out for what else is being published, think of yourself as a product that others need to invest in rather than just a wordsmith, and I would be surprised if you did not feel a greater ability to describe your publishing idea in more strategic terms. And with this new-found ability lies a much greater chance of appearing in print.

11

The questionnaire

Mark yourself on a scale of 1–10 where 1 indicates that you can barely get out of bed and 10 means you are pushing your bed down the high treet in search of a publisher.

1 Just how much do you want to see your book in print?

1	2	3	4	5	6	7	8	9	10

2 How much do other people like reading what you write?

1	2	3	4	5	6	7	8	9	10

3 How creative are you?

1	2	3	4	5	6	7	8	9	10

4 How strong are your personal support mechanisms?

1	2	3	4	5	6	7	8	9	10

5 How well-established is you writing habit?

1	2	3	4	5	6	7	8	9	10

6 Do you have something to write about that others would want to read?

1	2	3	4	5	6	7	8	9	10

7 How confident are you to present yourself as a writer?

1	2	3	4	5	6	7	8	9	10

8 How positively do you respond to rejection?

1	2	3	4	5	6	7	8	9	10

9 How well-read are you?

1	2	3	4	5	6	7	8	9	10

10 How much do you know about the publishing industry?

1	2	3	4	5	6	7	8	9	10

Total:

12

What your score means

As a teenager I loved the quizzes that appeared in magazines. If you got mostly 'a's it meant one thing; mostly 'c's, another. Sometimes my friends and I would read the category descriptions at the end, decide which one we wanted to belong to, and shape our answers accordingly.

I am afraid that the questionnaire you have just filled in is not like that. It's not possible to read the questions, respond, add up your score and then decide which one of three categories you fit into. Your responses are part of something much more complicated.

The questions you have answered are meant to be issues that you think about in detail, and take to heart. What is more, I have suggested that you do not regard the answers you give now as final. Some of the questions asked will have raised issues that you may not have examined before, so I recommend that you think about them again in three or six months' time, and then review your progress.

Understanding your total score

You will have come up with a total, but before we consider what that means, you need to be honest with yourself about the frame of mind in which you completed your answers.

You will have seen from the questionnaire that you can have a second stab at the answers after a few months, so you need to ask yourself if this affected the way in which you responded. Did you downplay your achievements, confident that you can improve, or give yourself a total for where you think you are right now? A low overall score could be a method of motivating yourself to think about these areas more in future, or it could imply that there is a huge amount of work to be done that you are not yet ready for.

Professional authors with whom I have tested this questionnaire all agreed that the questions are valid and are important if you are going to be published. Those who are already in print usually get at least 75%.

A low overall score (say, 40%) could be a method of helping yourself think about these areas in future – or it could imply that there is much to do.

Which questions are most important?

The questionnaire puts ten issues in front of you and asks you to think about each one in detail. Inevitably, some are more important than others, and your own particular areas of weakness are those you need to work on. Sometimes consciousness of a weakness in one area will encourage you to compensate in another. For example, I met a writer recently whose first novel was crafted at a time of immense personal trauma – her husband had left and she was coping as a single parent with a demanding job. This fuelled her desire to get into print, and each evening, once her daughter had gone to bed, she sat down to write. She finished the first draft of her novel in six weeks. Similarly, the world is full of people who can write very well, and dream of writing a book, but lack the determination – or the self-confidence – to take themselves sufficiently seriously and push to get into print. Those running Creative Writing courses have often commented that it's not necessarily the most talented writers who get best known, but those with the strongest drive.

If pressed as to which questions matter most, I think it would be very difficult to achieve publication without high scores in question one (how much do you want to do this?), question five (how well-established is your writing habit?), and question seven (how well do you take rejection?). Your determination to get into print is crucial; if you do not have a writing habit, there will be nothing to print; and all writers have to face rejection – it's what you do afterwards that matters. Picking yourself up again and keeping going is vital if you are going to get published.

13

Is there *not* a book in you?

If you got a low overall score on the questionnaire, and cannot justify the marks you gave yourself as a subconscious (or conscious) attempt to push yourself on to achieve more, you are perhaps beginning to think you may not have a book in you. This can be hard to accept.

Some people nurse the ambition to get into print for years. Whenever they hear of a new author, and their substantial advance, they wince and look for reasons why the success that has eluded them has been awarded to someone else. Is the lucky person younger, prettier, male/female, gay/straight, blacker/whiter, more popular or simply better connected? Others are vastly more proactive and fire off submission after unsuccessful submission; it appears that there is a competition for the number of rejections you can boast of once you do get published – best-selling author James Patterson quotes 37 rejections, before the 38th publisher he approached took him on.

Whether or not you achieve publication, one thing that would-be writers do find difficult is accepting that perhaps, just perhaps, writing talent is not equally distributed; that some people really do write better than they do. In 2002, the *Daily Mail* hosted a seminar at the London Book Fair on how to get published. It sold out quickly and more than 200 people paid £40 each to attend for the day. At the very end of the seminar there was a question-and-answer session, during which one delegate put the following:

"I have sent out my manuscript 20 times and still had no positive feedback. What should I do now?"

There was a long silence, and then agent Carole Blake gave the answer that several were thinking but not brave enough to say:

"Has it occurred to you that you cannot write?"

Sometimes you can be so sustained by your writing fantasy that each new rejection seems utterly exasperating; but a cycle of immense highs followed by desperate lows is not good for one's long-term health or mental stability. In these circumstances it can be a huge relief to turn to someone else for an objective opinion on your writing chances. Literary consultant Rebecca Swift commented:

> "We engage with the writing, openly and honestly, with a strong understanding of what they are trying to achieve, but with sufficient experience of the industry and other writers' work to spot if someone is being derivative without knowing it, or simply banal. Some writers absorb our feedback and then come back two years later with a much stronger manuscript; others find the feedback a huge relief and move on to do other things. I remember one man in particular. He wrote us an agonised letter in which he described his passionate desire to write, yet how bogged down he felt in the process of trying to achieve publication; he felt he had no objectivity about his work left. We engaged with the work, but gave him straightforward feedback, which was what he asked for. He said our report had 'saved him years of struggle'."

Having taken a serious look at the issues detailed in this book, you may now feel that you could cut yourself some slack, and perhaps decide that trying to get published is not for you. This may give you lots of extra spare time, allow you to reconnect with your family and friends, enable you to spot the satisfaction you have up to now overlooked in your day job, or discover other opportunities you have to be creative.

Most of us are creative on a daily basis; it's just that we don't give ourselves credit for it. I gave a few suggestions of how else to feel creative in the opening chapter, and most were fairly obvious (grow things, make new friends, etc.). I want to use this final chapter of the book to provide examples of how some people derive a feeling of creativity from doing things other than writing, and tips on how to do this yourself.

As I researched this part of the book, one idea emerged with particular force. Creative satisfaction often arrives through *being able to identify the difference that you make personally to a situation or relationship*. Being able to spot your role in shaping something, even if it is part of something else that is vast and bureaucratic, seems the essence of feeling that you have a choice – and if you have a choice, you have the basis of self-determination. When plans are imposed, and we have no ability to negotiate or depart from the established system, the individual can feel disempowered and demoralised.

My degree was in Fine Arts and History, and I remember studying the architect Le Corbusier. His *Unité d'Habitation*, a long block of flats whose external surface oscillated in a fascinating manner, achieved iconic status in the early 20th century. Ironically though, it apparently induced a high incidence of depression among individual residents, who could not spot where they lived from the outside. I related this story to a university student recently, who lived in a high-rise block of university flats, and he said he put a candle in his window for precisely that reason – so that from the outside of the anonymous tower block he could see where he lived. This is a good metaphor for thinking about creativity. If you can point to your bit in the overall plan, you are able to feel that you are a creative individual.

There follows a series of interviews with people doing a variety of different jobs. I asked them which bits of their job gave them the most satisfaction – if they could identify 'how they made a difference'. The responses may surprise you, as they did me.

Software Team Engineer – Sylvia Rowland

I work in the IT industry, although I have a background in business, and my job is spotting mistakes in programs and trying to help with a solution. I run tests to establish if there are errors and what we can do to fix the situation if problems arise. That does not sound terribly exciting, but in reality the 'people skills' I need to help me with this, and the care and sensitivity I have to exercise, mean this is a very exacting job!

Just imagine how you would feel if you had just built a wall, and someone came along and, not liking one brick, suggested that the whole thing had to go. My job is to establish what is wrong, and then tactfully point out how the situation could be rescued – not by knocking it all down, but by isolating the problem and working towards a possible solution.

People who work in IT on systems and software design can get really into their work – and out of the habit of communicating with other humans. My job is to find a helpful way of enabling all parties to understand the problem, without anyone feeling under-valued in the process. I think the fact that I have a background in business helps – all those years of team-working are an asset – but my guiding principle is always to think, how would I want to hear this news? If I manage to get a point across, and everyone feels encouraged to carry on working towards a solution, then I feel a great sense of achievement.

Builder – Jack Paterson
(jpatersonbuilders@blueyonder.co.uk)

I have been running a firm of builders for 25 years. It's hard work, and physically demanding, but I've always believed that anything that is worth achieving does not come easily. Money is not every-thing, but seeing buildings finished and being used and enjoyed makes me feel very proud.

The team is very important. We place a lot of emphasis on the team working together, and I like people to be able to do lots of things. Whatever needs doing, we all need to get on with it, and we all need to know where a job is going. It's a bit like conducting an orchestra: I may be waving my arms about, but if the players are not with me we are going nowhere. I believe very firmly in the importance of praise, and passing on the credit, but if people are happy to accept a pat on the back they must also be able to take it when things are not good enough.

I also get quite involved with the client, and get to know them as people rather than as just those who pay the bills. If you get to know them as people, you can often do a better job, making suggestions as you go along.

My favourite bit is digging the foundations. Without strong foundations you can't do much in life, and seeing the foundations for a really good building in place gives me pleasure. I like standing in the hole and looking up at where the building will go. Once the concrete is poured on top, you have a really solid start – provided you have done the right things underneath. I also like it when we come up with additional ideas that were not in the plans, for example suggesting how a spare corner could be used or changing the position of a door to give a room more sensible proportions. Sometimes you can only come up with these ideas once the project is starting to exist in three dimensions.

Buildings usually come out better than the plans, and seeing a finished space that is warm, used and appreciated is great. I love it when clients say thank you.

Chartered Surveyor – Alex Stevens, GVA Grimley LLP

I am a chartered surveyor but I spend most of my time looking for loopholes in taxation legislation to minimise our clients' operating costs.

Business rates were established in 1603 and almost all business property has a rateable value. Chartered surveyors working with business clients try to save them money on what they spend on business rates. There are two ways of doing this. Either you can look for a reduction in the valuation of the property (which of course is a risk because it could go up as well as down), or you look for opportunities to minimise liability by spotting mistakes in the legislation. These can be exploited to the clients' advantage. I have no moral difficulty with this as the legislation is always established and interpreted to the Revenue's advantage, with no consideration for those who are providing large quantities of governmental income, and in that sense they have an unfair advantage. Any business should try to minimise their overheads.

When I find these loopholes – and it's usually through being good at detail, and thinking laterally about the interpretation of words – I market them to both our existing clients and to those of our competitors. It is vastly intellectually satisfying and makes me feel on the ball. Sometimes we gain a short lead-time, and others pick up on what we have noticed. But even a lead-time of three months before either our competitors spot the benefits we have seen, or the government changes the legislation, can be enough to save our clients hundreds of thousands of pounds and in some cases millions of pounds. I am self-employed and love having the freedom to do what I want when I want to do it. Perhaps a thank you from the client gives me most satisfaction.

Energy Consultant – Richard Montgomery

I work for Shell and currently spend the working week in The Hague, coming back to London at weekends. My job involves lots of meetings, and a lot of travel, but I can be quite specific about the thing that motivates me.

I like putting together large deals, and handling the arrangements. Making an agreement in the oil and gas business is an immensely time-consuming process. There has to be trust; both sides have to be satisfied with the deal in order to stick to it, and you have to try to anticipate all the problems that might arise further down the process, when perhaps political or environmental conditions might have changed. The situation is further complicated because I am making arrangements for the supply of gas, and so there has to be a formal agreement in place before any of the extraction and supply processes can begin. It's not like oil, where the physical product can be extracted and shipped around the world until it finds a buyer. Gas is more nebulous; its delivery is much more costly and it is not an easily re-saleable commodity, so all aspects of extraction and delivery have to be tied up before anything moves forward.

This takes a big capacity for detail, a good memory and careful planning. And as a result of what I do, I feel motivated by the fact that large numbers of people will have access to a clean fuel that will keep them warm well into the future. For example, one agreement that I spent a lot of time brokering in 1998 only started producing gas in 2004 and will carry on delivering energy long after I have retired. My part in this process feels very satisfying.

VT Editor – Brian Harper-Lewis

I'm a freelance editor working mainly for Discovery Channel and Ascent Media. I work on programmes ranging from the highly stimulating (e.g. *Madrid* and *The Plane That Fought Back* about the terrorist atrocities) to the delightful (e.g. a beautifully photographed recent series on India) and the unashamedly populist (e.g.

Monster Garage, Fashion Avenue, Fishing, and radical makeover programmes involving plastic surgery). The work can frequently be 10–12 hours at a stretch, with only minimal breaks for snacks or the loo. Lunch tends to get forgotten regularly.

I find my work utterly absorbing. I can be so glued to it that I barely notice the passing of time. It demands my complete attention and there's an immense satisfaction that comes from absolute concentration. Even when the programmes I'm working on are a tad obvious, I find that the craft processes, and trying to do one's best at speed, keeps me motivated and involved. I never get bored.

Perhaps I might have been advised to have sought a more linear career path within a large organisation, but by now that would have meant full-time commitment and the probability of spending life behind a desk, or in meetings, rather than honing things people watch. Making programmes can be a little like trying to play three-dimensional chess at speed: sometimes frustrating, occasionally annoying, but always engaging. Helping achieve the best for what appears on screen has consistently been important to me. While freelance life can be unpredictable, one genuinely has the ability to say 'no', and opt to spend time fiddling about with boats, surprise journeys and the delights of family. So why do I so frequently say yes?

How did I get into this? Years ago, still a schoolboy, I read an article on the future of broadcasting, the essence of which was: 'A key to the future is the creation of lasting and repeatable imagery.' At the time, I wrote it up on my wall, and still think it's true. A significant component of job satisfaction is knowing that one has tried to do the best one can, whatever the programme or purpose. Is that passion? I find I still love it when a programme really comes together.

At the end of a day (or night) in an edit suite I'm frequently exhausted but elated, often arriving back home only to rave to my lovely but long-suffering partner about arcane details of the programmes I've been working on.

Sometimes it's something I am proud to know, sometimes something I might wish I did not now know, but it's always fascinating.

Health Club Manager – Wendy Orr, West Woods Health Club, Edinburgh

I run a sports centre – I am the General Manager. Our membership covers a wide range of people, from school children to very senior citizens.

I probably play less sport now that I am busy with my job, but still feel it is so important to keep fit. When you are tired or feeling stressed it can be tempting just to go home and relax, but in fact taking exercise ups your energy level; you get a sense of achievement through working towards goals. Exercise gives you a lift and you feel more alert, and more focused. I find I feel more tired if I *don't* do any exercise. Exercise is relaxing partly because you have to switch your mind on to something else; it's difficult to think about work as you are using a running machine or following the instructions of the person leading the class. And forgetting about what has been occupying your brain all day is very relaxing.

People usually join a health club with a specific goal in mind: maybe they want to get thinner for a wedding, to look better on the beach, or perhaps their doctor has advised that they should get some exercise. We draw up a training programme to suit their requirements. When you encourage them, particularly those who are hesitant about getting started, then see them looking fitter and more positive week by week, you feel a real sense of achievement. I also like to see clients chatting in the café afterwards. I think the social side of exercise is very important and like to think they are making new friends and feeling more socially confident in the process. Of course it is their effort that gets them to the goal they want to achieve, but I love feeling part of the process; I can really feel we have made a difference to people's lives.

Full-time mother

I did a law degree and worked in general litigation until I was heavily pregnant with my first child. I have not had a full-time job since, and my two children are now aged 14 and 12. I am about to return to work, three days a week.

To start with the role of full-time mother was a bit of a shock to the system. Both my husband and I are only-children and neither of us had large extended families. I found having day-long contact with a small baby or child that you could not rationalise with pretty frustrating; I enjoyed their company much more as they got older.

I did not particularly want to go back to law, but the job you do does have a big impact on how society values you, and people do tend to place a different value on you if you are giving your time for nothing. Since my children were seven and five I have been involved in volunteer roles – most particularly using my experience of arbitration to work for an organisation of lay conciliators.

Women obviously struggled long and hard to be accepted within the workplace, but I do feel that liberation is about choice – and that should include deciding *not* to be part of the workplace.

It has been very important for me that *I* decided to do this. It was my choice rather than being forced upon me; if a decision is consciously made it is much easier to live with. My priorities changed when I had a family. Choice is never unfettered, there are always consequences you have to live with, but accepting that it was your decision to do something is really important, I think.

Secondly I really value the support of my friends in a similar position. Those I met through the NCT I am still in touch with, and keeping up-to-date with the situations we face in personal and parenting roles has become very important. There is a lot of encouragement and support around if you tap into it.

Finally, my role at home has always been upheld by my husband. We do eat together as a family, and spend time together, and he has always viewed what I do as a vital in 'holding the whole thing together' rather than just 'being at home'. It helps that we have the same attitude to income, in that whatever comes into the house, whoever earns it, belongs to both of us.

Teacher – Julie Kelford

The main thing I love about teaching is the variety it offers. Each day is different. I also like the versatility it requires of me. There is the practical side of teaching – explaining things to the children and then encouraging them to do them; and the theory behind it, which continues to fascinate me. I work in the reception class, so the majority of children arrive unable to read and write, and by the end of the year they can – so it's easy to feel a sense of achievement. I am particularly motivated by working with children who find it difficult; changing a child's attitude from being resistant to feeling proud of their achievement is important. I often encourage them to dwell on how far they have come ('Do you remember how you used to not like writing? Well just look at what you can do now.').

The other main 'plus' about being a teacher is working within a team; people outside the profession tend not to realise what a collaborative group we are. We are not in competition with each other, and we work as a team (or should do) to achieve the goals that have been set. The constant changing of these goals due to new government initiatives can be very trying, but the team response makes them bearable. Yes it's hard work, and we do a lot of work in the holidays, but there is huge solidarity within teaching: we really do support each other.

Community Nurse – Nicola Whitwell

I work as a community nurse in the area where I live. Every trainee nurse has to do a spell in community nursing and as this was the bit I enjoyed the most, I decided to make this my speciality.

The main thing I love about my job is the variety – no day is the same as another. Much of my work is giving support to families who are supporting terminally ill patients at home – many more people decide they would like to die at home these days, rather than in hospital, and so my job is to make this as easy as possible for them. I also look after patients who have just come out of hospital – patients tend to stay in for much shorter times than they used to, and so need nursing support and help once they get home. As well as dealing with the practicalities of care, I advise on how to access other services.

Part of the satisfaction comes from knowing what to do; managing pain and being a source of up-to-date information. I find that patients today are much better informed than they used to be, and so I place a strong emphasis on keeping myself up-to-date, through training and reading the latest research in the nursing press. If I explain medical processes well to patients, even when the outcome is not likely to be positive, it boosts their confidence in the management of the condition when I am not there, and this gives me satisfaction. I also enjoy involvement with the families.

Arts Administrator – Karen Mountney, Director of the Children's Programme, Edinburgh Book Festival

I don't think of myself as an especially creative person, and I'm certainly not writing a novel – or thinking of doing so. I've been involved in arts marketing, administration and programming for over ten years now, and for me the job satisfaction comes from enabling people to get together; in this case connecting writers with their audience. I have always been a great reader and I think there are huge benefits to reading, such as developing understanding, emotional intelligence and empathy as well as the more obvious benefits of literacy, communication skills and self-expression. I get a lot of satisfaction from giving children the opportunity to engage with writers and explore their own creativity at the same time. My degree was in sociology and psychology and I was always interested in the social and behavioural aspects of communication, reading and writing. I have to read an enormous number of children's books as part of my job and I get a huge amount of pleasure from having access to so many high-quality books.

I love seeing the first copies of the printed programme. It presents in a nutshell all the plans and ideas we had, all the to-ing and fro-ing to set it up, all the fundraising and planning venues in which to stage things. When you see the printed programme there is a real sense of everything starting to happen, which is exciting.

I can only see a small cross-section of events – I maybe see ten full events (we put on 263 children's events this year), which is tiny. But I do talk to the speakers before and after events, and of course I am in touch with them in the planning stages – and to thank them afterwards. I like the knowing lots of interesting people that goes with this job – it's lovely when you go to other events and festivals and meet people who say they enjoy taking part in Edinburgh International Book Festival!

Cook

I have tried to write a book for children several times now. Each time I got as far as writing the text, circulating it to friends who work in publishing and looking at their feedback, but something has always held me back from trying to push it any further and I do feel this is a lack of the final confidence. I just don't have the self-belief to keep pushing, which is I know what I ought to do.

I find my creative outlet in cooking. When I am cooking I lose everything else I am worried about; it all goes. I am not one for listening to the radio while I do it – the thinking and physical actions are enough for me. My favourite parts are the planning and presentation – the bits at either end of the process. I love thinking about what to cook for people; what will delight them. In particular I love making light and airy puddings such as mousses and pavlovas.

I also love presenting food to make it look as attractive and appetising as possible – thinking about the colour, the dish it will sit in and what it will look like on the table.

Sales Assistant – Roya Henry

I have always liked working with people and explaining things. Before I had my children I worked for a pharmaceutical company in sales, so I think selling was always something I was good at. I then stopped for ten years and stayed at home. I now work three mornings a week at a department store in our nearest large town. I work on the perfume counter.

I really enjoy matching customers and perfumes – this gives me big satisfaction. Customers come in looking for advice and I like matching people with what I know they will enjoy. Just today a woman came in – she has two teenaged daughters – and wanted to buy each of them a perfume for Christmas. We talked about the image they found attractive and she also wanted to be able to tolerate the scent herself – after all, she has to sit in the car with them. Thinking about what is stylish to 14- and 16-year-old girls was interesting for me (I have two boys) and we matched their interests to what I could offer her. Sending her on her way with two purchases, but also two solutions, gave me a good sense of achievement.

I also love it when customers I have served return and let me know that the purchase they made (with joint effort) was appropriate. Once they feel they can trust me, they proceed to ask for all sorts of other advice!

Mature student

I took retirement three years early from a policy and management job within the Civil Service.

I have had a lifelong interest in history, and embarked on a part-time degree in the subject at Kingston University – a six-year commitment initially. But after a short while I found the subject so engrossing that I transferred to studying full-time.

I am finding the course desperately satisfying. I now find myself reading – and writing – history from an analytic viewpoint, and I have learnt how to do historical research. For someone who has read as much history as I have over the years, this is very satisfying. I plan to carry on studying now I have started, with an MA and then perhaps a PhD.

My wife has commented that I seem much more relaxed and confident, and I am happy that I am carrying on using my brain, rather than just playing golf!

Gardener – Mark Brunsdon, mbgardencare@aol.com

There is nothing I like better than being able to create something lovely out of a mess – and the bigger the mess to begin with, the more I like it. I have just been involved in cutting back a wilderness, and in the process found a greenhouse that the client did not know they had – you can imagine what state the garden was in for that to happen! I like doing a good clear-out, and my favourite job is pulling ivy down, from a wall or garden fence – I think it is so destructive of masonry and blocks other plants, so I am always pleased when a client asks me to do that.

I love coming up with designs in my head, and find a real sense of achievement in seeing it through in practice. Quite often I get so lost in what I am doing that I lose all track of time; it can be frustrating when you have to leave something half done, but time pressure means that I sometimes have to do that – otherwise I would be late for my next client. I like to complete things and realise I am a perfectionist. Once I built a pergola for someone and the horizontal beam was not right. They had not noticed, but it bothered me, and so I fixed it the next time I went back.

I love seeing change. Sometimes people just ask me to mow the lawn and that's fine, but what I really like is to look at a garden at the end of a job and see the difference I have made. Then I can really say to myself, 'that was a "worth-it"day'.

Hairdresser – Julie Moss

Hairdressing is physically tiring. You are on your feet all day, and there is a constant time pressure – you have to be a good manager to get everyone done in the available time. In my case, because I am moving from house to house, time management can be even more difficult due to things beyond my control – like my children getting ill at school or traffic jams.

Having your hair done means that in the process you do not look your best – with your hair wet, or with bits of it in tinfoil, you do not look as you normally do to visitors (or even friends). So for the time that I am in a client's house I often take over answering the door. I sign for parcels, let people in or out, and tell people calling to fix something what to do – and all because my client will let me see them in a mess, but does not want to be seen by others like that!

I think it is this short-lived vulnerability that seems to bring about an intimacy between client and stylist, and I suspect we chat in a way that either party would not do so openly with other people. I feel very protective towards them and would never break a confidence.

Everyone likes to do something nice for someone, and my job offers me the chance to do that on a daily basis. I love it when I leave someone looking great when their hair looked a mess when I arrived, and even more so when they are pleased with the effect.

Literary Consultant – Rebecca Swift

My parents are both creatives: one is a writer, the other an actor. I worked in publishing after leaving university, but found the edging-out of editors, in favour of marketing people, dispiriting. What I enjoyed about publishing was engaging creatively with texts and working with strong ideas and writers who were good and important – even if these did not sell in vast numbers. Editors could make more choices than they can now. Often, those writers an editor backed when they were "small fry" went on to become more commercially mainstream – but what worries me now is that they may never get that chance.

I do write myself – poetry, journalism and an opera libretto, for example – but founding TLC (The Literary Consultancy) has given me the opportunity to be creative in ways I really didn't anticipate. It is exciting to hear back from people that, simply because we are there and can engage in depth but not in too naïve a way, we can make a real difference. After running TLC for a few years, we got a grant to be able to give free help to low-income writers and also to do a tour asking questions about the publishing industry. I regularly give talks on what I do. It feels fresh and exciting. I never quite know what will happen next. It doesn't completely mean either that one gives up on writing, but these days it doesn't pay to be unrealistic. It can also be a great mistake ignoring certain sources of creative engagement with the world at the expense of another.

Dentist – Jill Hansel

I am a dentist. If I get asked at parties what my job is, the most common response is, "I don't like dentists." Whereas when I was younger this used to make me hesitant about talking about what I do, these days I feel much more confident.

There are many things that I enjoy about my job. The first is the fact that I can usually put something right in a short space of time. If a patient comes in with pain, more often than not I can sort it out within the time allotted, and that makes both of us feel good. I find particular satisfaction in working with nervous patients – reassuring them that there is nothing to be frightened of and building their confidence. In more recent years I have become involved in cosmetic dentistry – which has a far lower entry point than you might imagine; it's not just for Hollywood! This too is satisfying. Often I am working with patients who have felt self-conscious about their teeth for years, and worried about their smile. With careful treatment you can improve both the look of their teeth, and how they see themselves – and that can really make me feel that I have made a difference.

If you mention the word "dentist", most people think of a one-off visit to a place they would rather not be. But as a dentist I have the chance to build long-term relationships with patients I really get to know, and I enjoy that.

Part-time student – Moira Wilson

I always wanted to do a history degree. I did not go to university after school but the ambition was always in the back of my mind. I set myself a target of starting when my child started school, and in that year I embarked on a part-time history degree, which would take six years. I am now in year four.

For me, the chance to study provides a new outlet; a chance to develop a different aspect of myself. I work two days a week in the health service, and have found that study has increased my confidence in general and the respect with which I am treated at work. I am using my brain more, which is very satisfying. My family and friends have also commented that I tend to be more reasoned in my behaviour since I started the degree. I think that means that I am better at seeing both sides of an argument these days!

Friend – Kris Stuchbury writes about her mother, Glen Checkland

My mother was a teacher, although she stopped working to look after my sister and I when we were little. Later on, she went back to part-time work in a teacher–training college.

A turning point was reached when we left home and she had to decide whether to increase her hours or do something else. She eventually decided to put her energies into the home. My father was a professor at a university and was hugely successful in his field; she felt fully part of his achievement. We also had a number of relatives and friends for whom life was difficult for various reasons, and she decided that instead of working full time, she would maintain communication with people – make herself available to others, rather than being over-busy and not having time. She used to keep in touch by visiting people, often some way away and by writing long, chatty and supportive letters.

She had had an unhappy childhood herself and considered herself to have been very fortunate in later life. She was not religious, but believed in the "collective human unconscious"; this was a way of passing on her good fortune to others. She had a great deal of energy and other people appreciated her care and love. My friends were often surprised when, if they wrote a letter to her to thank her for a visit, or to tell her about something, she would reply – and I know they appreciated contact with her. She was a remarkable woman. Her achievements are summed up most appropriately in the last paragraph of Middlemarch:

> "Her full nature, like that river of which Cyrus broke the strength, spent itself in channels which had no great name on the earth. But the effect of her being on those around her was incalculably diffusive: for the growing good of the world is partly dependent on unhistoric acts; and that things are not so ill with you and me as they might have been, is half owing to the number who lived faithfully a hidden life and rest in unvisited tombs."

Overall comment on these quotations

Some of these quotes are from people you would not think of as occupying creative jobs, and yet their ability to spot the point at which they can make a choice, and to highlight the difference that they make, is tangible. All are being creative. Spotting that you have choices and can be creative can boost your sense of self-worth. I think this is a really useful model for would-be writers to consider.

> "The publishing market is really difficult these days, and too unpredictable. Are you really going to put all your self-worth in the hands of conglomerate publishing firms, which don't care primarily about you as a writer? It may be a case of, so what if they don't want to publish it? It does not mean it is without merit, and there are other ways of getting your work heard, like giving a reading, forming a writing circle and discussing your work, self-publishing or publishing it through local papers. I heard a poet read recently, at an event I was giving. His reading was electric and I will remember it far

longer than many of the published novels I read. He made a huge impression on us all."

Rebecca Swift

"While many people should be encouraged to write, having a book published in the UK trade is not the be all and end all, the standard by which the project's success is measured. Writing for oneself, one's family or friends can be an end in itself."

Francis Bickmore, Canongate

How to spot and take pleasure in what you are good at

1 Have a helicopter view of what your profession, industry or hobby is trying to achieve. Thus librarians are in the business of encouraging people to read; builders are in the business of providing better living or working space; sandwich shops are in the business of filling hunger – and providing diversion – and wedding dress shops are in the business of realising dreams. Hobbies and how you spend your time at home can be equally significant: thus reading widely makes you a more empathetic person; looking after children helps them grow into more rounded adults; thinking about how your home is decorated and maintained is part of making a welcoming and supportive atmosphere for your friends and/or family.

The most lowly job, seen from the point of view of the organisation's wider endeavour, can appear motivating. There is a story told of President Kennedy being shown around Cape Canaveral, and pausing to ask a cleaner what his job was. "Helping to put a man on the moon," was the swift reply.

2 Think how your role fits into the wider picture.

3 Consider what would happen if you did not do your bit.

4 Can you think of an example of you doing your job and someone commenting, positively or negatively? Determine how this made you feel

5 Which bits of your role give you the most satisfaction?

6 Do you time your day with any awareness of when you are doing the bits you like most? Doing the things that make you feel good first, or at a time in the day when you feel best able to tackle them, can substantially affect your sense of achievement. Consider whether it would make the day more enjoyable if you did so.

7 Congratulate yourself afterwards on how you did a good job.

8 Do you pass on praise to other people? Recognising an individual's contribution – whether it is your own or someone else's – plays a key part in motivation. I tend to feel that what goes around, comes around, and that if you comment yourself on other people's performance, the positive vibes in the workplace environment improve and everyone feels encouraged – and more likely to comment.

> "Next to physical survival, the greatest need of a human being is psychological survival – to be understood, to be affirmed, to be validated, to be appreciated."
>
> Stephen R Covey (see bibliography)

Interestingly, everyone I spoke to about their job said afterwards they had enjoyed the experience of talking about what they did well. Perhaps we should all lose some of this horrible British modesty and congratulate ourselves a little more on what we do well. Even if, in the process, we admit that it may not publish a book.

Conclusion

A few years ago my mother bought me a Liberty diary for Christmas. It was covered in Liberty print and contained cream paper of a beautiful quality; I can still remember how smooth it felt. Glancing through it, near the front, I noticed two pages of information on first aid. And amidst all the advice on how to treat sprains and burns, up popped a paragraph on 'Emergency Childbirth'. Sadly I no longer have the book to refer to, but from memory it went something like this:

Boil water. Get plenty of clean towels. When the head appears ...

Having had four children by the time I read this advice, it seemed to me that there was rather more involved in the delivering of children, even in a hurry.

This book is a similarly brief guide for writers on how to consider publication. It skates over the surface, offers generalisations, doesn't get involved in parts of the process that may go on for years, and tries to reach conclusions about processes that are, by their very condition, nebulous and hard to define. As work has progressed, however, I have become increasingly convinced that it does have a purpose. What is more, the many writers who have become involved – either through testing the questionnaire or providing feedback on their own writing processes – have said that my list tells them important things about themselves; things that they had not necessarily identified before.

The most surprising outcome was finding out just how uniform were the responses of the writing community. Establishing that so many writers felt the same way as I did was part encouraging – I suddenly felt involved in a much wider community – but part dispiriting (just why do we all go on if there are so many knock-backs?).

Whether you decide you are going to push for publication, remain a writer for your own pleasure, or give up the ambition to have a book in print, I hope my advice and that of the myriad contributors to this work, has been useful.

Alison Baverstock, June 2006

Bibliography

Becoming a Writer, Dorothea Brande (most recent edition 1996, Macmillan, Basingstoke), with a foreword by Malcolm Bradbury – a classic, first published in 1934 and still uniquely helpful. This is a marvellous book, with real insight into the creative process, and a conclusion whose effect compares with the sublime state induced by high opera's best moments. The new foreword by Malcolm Bradbury is particularly useful. If you read nothing else on this area, read this.

The Courage to Write, Ralph Keyes, Henry Holt and Company, New York, 1995

Creative Writing: a practical guide, Julia Casterton, second edition, Macmillan, Basingstoke, 1998

The Creative Writing Coursebook, edited by Julia Bell and Paul Magrs, from the University of East Anglia, Macmillan, Basingstoke, 2001

The Creative Writing Handbook, edited by John Singleton and Mary Luckhurst, Palgrave, London, 2000

Feel the Fear and Do It Anyway: How to turn your fear and indecision into confidence and action, Susan Jeffers, Arrow Books, London 1991

From Pitch to Publication, Carole Blake, Macmillan, Basingstoke 1999

How Not to Write a Novel, David Armstrong, Allison and Busby London 2003

On Writing, Stephen King, Hodder and Stoughton, London, 2000

Reading, Writing and Leaving Home: Life on the page, Lynn Freed, Harcourt, New York 2005
Teaching Students to Write, Beth S Neman, OUP, Oxford, 1995

Rotten Rejections, Bill Henderson, Pushcart Press, New York, 1990

The 7 Habits of Highly Effective People: Powerful lessons in personal change, Stephen R Covey, Simon and Schuster, 1989

Understanding Style, Joe Glaser, OUP Inc, New York, 1999

The Writing Book, Kate Grenville, Allen and Unwin, 1990, Australia

A&C Black Writers' Guides Series
Developing Characters for Script Writing, Rib Davis
Freelance Copywriting, Diana Wimbs
Freelance Writing for Newspapers, Jill Dick
Ghostwriting, Andrew Crofts
Marketing Your Book: An Author's Guide, Alison Baverstock
Writing Biography & Autobiography, Brian D. Osborne
Writing Comedy, John Byrne
Writing Crime Fiction, H.R.F. Keating
Writing Dialogue for Scripts, Rib Davis
Writing Fantasy and Science Fiction, Lisa Tuttle
Writing for Magazines, Jill Dick
Writing a Play, Steve Gooch
Writing Poetry, John Whitworth
Writing Popular Fiction, Rona Randall

Writing Romantic Fiction, Daphne Clair and Robyn Donald
Writing Sitcoms, John Byrne and Marcus Powell
Writing Successful Textbooks, Anthony Haynes

Other A & C Black books for writers
Novel Writing, Evan Marshall
The Reader's Encyclopedia, William Rose Benét
Research for Writers, Ann Hoffmann
The Weekend Novelist, Robert J. Ray and Bret Norris
Word Power: A Guide to Creative Writing, Julian Birkett
Writers' and Artists' Yearbook

List of writers who have contributed to this book

Nicholas Allan is the author/illustrator of more than 30 children's books. Several are bestsellers, including *The Queen's Knickers*, *Jesus' Christmas Party* and *Heaven*. *Hilltop Hospital* was adapted into a BAFTA-winning series for CITV. Nicholas is also the winner of the Sheffield Children's Book Award and the Red House Children's Book Award. His books have been published in over 20 languages.
www.nicholasallan.co.uk

Hedi Argent writes for children, professionals and families about many aspects of adoption, fostering and kinship care. Her books are published by the British Agencies for Adoption and Fostering (BAAF), and their website is www.baaf.org.uk

Trisha Ashley gave up her fascinating but time-consuming hobbies of house-moving and divorce some years ago in order to settle in North Wales, though her only claim to the area is a Welsh grandmother. After puzzling over which quarter of her is Welsh, she's decided it's probably her writing arm. Her books have been widely translated.
www.geocities.com/trisha_ashley2002

Sunil Badami was born in Sydney. He currently lives in London with his wife, completing a Masters in Creative and Life Writing at Goldsmiths College. He has written for a number of publications, and is currently writing his first novel.

Alison Baverstock worked in publishing before setting up a consultancy to offer training and good ideas within the industry. She also writes about publishing – and about life. www.alisonbaverstock.com

Hazel Broadfoot joined Watersone's in its infancy and managed several branches before joining the board. She became disenchanted with corporate life and is now co-owner of two successful independent bookshops in London: The Bookshop, Dulwich Village and Beckett's Bookshop. She can be contacted on 020 8693 2808.

Anne Brooke writes fiction and poetry and has been short-listed for both the Asham and Royal Literary Fund Awards. She has published a poetry collection, *Tidal*, and a novel, *The Hit List*, and is represented by agent, John Jarrold. In her spare time, she plays bad golf. Further details are at www.annebrooke.com or www.goldenford.co.uk

Emma Burstall is Features Editor of *Family Circle*, the national women's monthly magazine. Before that, she freelanced for a wide variety of publications including the *Daily Mail*, *Daily Telegraph*, *Sunday Mirror*, *Times Educational Supplement*, *New Woman*, *Woman* and *She*. She read English Literature at Cambridge University and lives in South West London with her husband and three children.

Brian Cathcart is the author of six books, including *Were You Still Up for Portillo?* (1997), *The Case of Stephen Lawrence* (1999) – which won the Crime Writers' Association Non-Fiction Award and the Orwell Prize – and *The Fly in the Cathedral* (2004), an account of how the atom was split in Cambridge in 1932. He lectures in journalism at Kingston University and is also assistant editor of the *New Statesman*, so for the moment has little time for book-writing. Aged 49, he lives in North London.

Julie Cohen's first novel, the fun, sexy romance *Featured Attraction* (Mills & Boon Modern Extra, March 2006), was short-listed for two major awards before it was published. She has seven follow-up novels finished or in the works and also writes mainstream fiction and nonfiction. Usually, she's exhausted. Visit her website and blog at www.julie-cohen.com

Andrew Collins began his writing career as a journalist, then moved sideways into scriptwriting for television – first *Family Affairs*, Channel Five's first soap, then *EastEnders*. This led to his first sitcom, *Grass*, co-written with Simon Day. Book-wise, Andrew has written the official biography of Billy Bragg and the official history of Friends Reunited. His first memoir, *Where Did It All Go Right?* was a *Sunday Times* bestseller and the third volume in the series is due this year. He is currently film editor of *Radio Times* and broadcasts regularly on BBC 6 Music, Radio 2 and Radio 4.
www.wherediditallgoright.com

Sheila Cornelius responded to an ad in the BFI film library and this led to the research and writing of *New Chinese Cinema*, published in 2002 (Wallflower Press). She also contributed to an encyclopaedia and to China-related magazines. In December 2005 she became a full-time writer. She lives in London and her writing ranges from fiction to copy for commercial websites.
www.writewords.org.uk/sheila_cornelius

Andrew Crofts was described in the *Independent* as 'the king of modern ghosts'. He has published over 40 ghosted books and has written a novel, *Maisie's Amazing Maids* (Stratus Books 2001) with a ghostwriter as the central character. He is also the author of *The Freelance Writer's Handbook* (Piatkus 2002) and *Ghostwriting* (A&C Black 2004).
www.andrewcrofts.com

Molly Cutpurse Transgendered English author. Published Bibliography: *The Last Winter* and *A Life Lived*. Publisher: Publish America. Pareidolia often plays a part in her creative process. Her website is www.mollycutpurse.com

Emma Darwin's novel *The Mathematics of Love* is published by Headline Review and will be published by Wm. Morrow (USA) in 2007. She has also had success in several short fiction prizes. Emma lives in London, is studying for a PhD in Creative Writing, and will admit to being a great-great-grand-daughter of Charles Darwin.
www.emmadarwin.com

Catherine Dell runs workshops on various aspects of oral communication, including presentation skills for authors who give readings of their work. Individual guidance is also available. She can be contacted at: Doggers London Road, Copdock, Ipswich, IP8 3JF, telephone: 01473 730293

Edward Denison is a heritage consultant, writer and architectural photographer working from the UK and China. For over six years he has worked with his partner, Guang Yu Ren, to document and promote under-represented architectural heritage with international organisations. Their written and photographic work has been published extensively worldwide and includes two seminal books on the architectural heritage of Asmara and Shanghai respectively.

Cathy Douglas has written a pop-sociology book, *The Superwoman Trap*, and a thriller, *Double Take*. She has co-written *The Bluffer's Guide to Men/Women* and (with Alison Baverstock), a distance-learning course on copywriting, plus endless blurbs, brochures, adverts and bus sides. In fact, she'll write pretty much anything that has words in it! You can contact her on 020 8858 7380.

Katie Fforde lives in Gloucestershire with her husband and some of her three children. Her hobbies are ironing and housework but, unfortunately, she has almost no time for them as she feels it her duty to keep a close eye on the afternoon chat shows.
www.randomhouse.co.uk

Jenny Haddon has written stories all her life. She is published in over 100 countries and 25 languages by Harlequin Mills and Boon under the pen name Sophie Weston. She was a member of the Romantic Novelists Association University Challenge team that made it to the finals in 2005. For her latest ventures, see her website www.jennyhaddon.com

Stephen Hancocks was a dentist before moving into dental writing, editing and publishing. This bolsters his real love – writing for performance, primarily theatre. His 'respectable' job is editor-in-chief of the *British Dental Journal*. He has his own publishing company and co-owns Outlaw Theatre Limited, for which he writes, performs and produces. www.shancoksltd.com

Gill Hines works as a freelance education consultant specialising in Health Education. This means that she takes on work from local authorities and schools around issues of health in the broader sense such as sex and relationships education and peer mediation. She runs a lot of training, works with pupils, staff and parents, and devises original materials both for teaching and training, including two commercially produced. She recently had her first book published, which she co-wrote with Alison Baverstock (*Whatever!*).

Heather Holden-Brown was an editor for 15 years at BBC Books and Headline. She worked with a range of fascinating people on their autobiographies, including Barbara Windsor, Sue MacGregor, Kate Adie and Hillary Rodham-Clinton. She now runs her own agency which represents writers of commercial non-fiction – in particular, journalism, history and politics, contemporary auto-biography and biography, entertainment and television, business, family memoir, cookery and diet. She can be contacted at heather@hhbagency.com

Margaret James is a journalist, novelist and freelance editor who has written 11 published novels and is a regular columnist on *Writing Magazine*. Margaret's latest contemporary novel is *Elegy*

for a Queen; her most recent historical novel *The Morning Promise* was published in 2005.
www.storytracks.net

PD James worked as a civil servant for many years, in the NHS and the Home Office, first in the Police Department and later in the Criminal Policy Department – all of which experience has been used in her novels. She has won many awards for crime writing. In 1997 she was elected President of the Society of Authors.

Meg Jensen is a New Yorker who received her Master's in English from New York University, and her PhD in English from University of London. She lectures in British and American Literature at Kingston University, where she is also head of the Department of Creative Writing. She came fifth in a family of six children and needs lots of attention.

Catherine Jones is an ex-army officer and member of the Romantic Novelists' Association; she has now written five novels with military backgrounds. She began writing by accident when asked to contribute to a magazine for fellow army wives, and since then has discovered a talent for observing the peculiarities of life with the Colours. She was short-listed for the Romantic Novel of the Year in 1999.

Bee Kenchington: after her family left home, much of her time was devoted to writing and publishing poetry, and she was short-listed for the role of Poet Laureate in West Sussex. Her only brother went down with *HMS Hood* in 1941 leaving 66 letters. Feeling that these had something to offer, she gave up poetry, wrote a commentary and published the letters under the title *... and home there's no returning*. The book came out when she was 81 and she is currently working on her second, another edited selection of family papers.

Bernard Lyall: after years shaping other people's stories as a television editor, Bernard Lyall is now making his own. The son of successful thriller-writer Gavin Lyall, he is working on his second 'first' novel, about an epic discovery which threatens to re-write human history, set among the graves of the Balkan wars.

Sharon Maas was born in Guyana and educated in England. After 30 years living in India and in Germany she settled in England to develop her writing career. Three of her novels are published by HarperCollins, London, and have been translated into four languages. Presently she is working on her fourth novel, *The Last of the Sugar Gods*.
www.sharonmaas.co.uk

Livi Michael has written four award-winning novels for adults; the *Frank and the Black Hamster of Narkiz* series for younger children, which was nominated for the Branford-Boase Award; *43 Bin St*, also for younger children; and *The Whispering Road*, which has been shortlisted for the Ottakers book award, the Stockton on Tees Children's Book of the Year Award, the Nestlé Prize, and was Borders USA Book of the Month in July 2005.

Nicola Morgan is an award-winning novelist for teenagers, author of *Mondays are Red*, *Fleshmarket*, *Sleepwalking* and *The Passionflower Massacre*. She has also written around 70 home-learning books, some *Thomas the Tank Engine* books, *The Leaving Home Survival Guide*, *Chicken Friend*, and *Blame My Brain*, an insight into the teenaged brain.
www.nicolamorgan.co.uk

Wendy Perriam was expelled from school for heresy, and then read History at Oxford. A series of offbeat jobs followed, ranging from artist's model to carnation disbudder, and she then embarked on a career in advertising. Having published 15 novels and three short-story collections, she feels that her many conflicting life experiences – strict convent-school discipline and swinging-sixties wildness, marriage and divorce, infertility and motherhood, 9-to-5 conformity and periodic Bedlam – have helped to shape her as a writer.
www.perriam.demon.co.uk

Gwyneth Pitt is Professor of Law and Dean of the Faculty of Business and Law at Kingston University. She researches and writes about employment and discrimination law. Her textbook, *Employment Law* (5th edition, Sweet & Maxwell 2003, 6th edition in preparation), is widely used on employment law courses in universities.

Adam Powley is the co-author, with Martin Cloake, of *We Are Tottenham*, published by Mainstream. More details at www.wearetottenhambook.com Adam has also contributed to the anthology *When Saturday Comes*, published by Penguin.

Philip Pullman's books have been widely praised. He has won the Whitbread Prize, the Carnegie Medal, The *Guardian* Children's Fiction Award, the Smarties Prize and the prize for Children's Book of the Year at the British Book Awards. The three volumes of the *His Dark Materials* trilogy have attracted enormous critical acclaim as well as making frequent appearances in the bestseller lists.
www.philip-pullman.com

John Ravenscroft lives in Lincolnshire, England and spends much of his time struggling to write fiction and co-editing *Cadenza Magazine*. His short stories have won prizes in various literary competitions and been published in dozens of magazines. His work has also been broadcast on the BBC.
www.johnravenscroft.co.uk

Jane Rogers has written seven novels including *Mr Wroe's Virgins* and *Promised Lands* (Writers' Guild Award 1996). She is editor of OUP's *Good Fiction Guide*. She also writes for TV and radio, and teaches on the Writing MA, Sheffield Hallam University. Her most recent book is *The Voyage Home*.
www.janerogers.org

Anne Rooney lives in Cambridge with two daughters but spends part of each year in Venice, Italy. She's a full-time children's writer, which sounds impressive but mostly entails stressing about deadlines and tracing obscure facts about seagull wine or robots that can burp. Her work colleague is a lobster called Marcel. www.annerooney.co.uk

Anne Rowe is a Senior Lecturer in English Literature at Kingston University. She is the Director of the Centre for Iris Murdoch Studies and Director of the Academic Skills Centre. She is author of *The Visual Arts and the Novels of Iris Murdoch*, and the European Editor of the *Iris Murdoch NewsLetter*. She is currently editing a collection of essays, *Iris Murdoch: A Reassessment* to be published in 2006. She divides her time between London and Crickhowell, Powys.

Anne Sebba was the first woman hired by Reuters on their graduate trainee scheme as a foreign correspondent. Although she never covered a war as a journalist, she wrote a book about women who did – *Battling for News*. She has written seven other books, including biographies of Mother Teresa and Laura Ashley and is currently working on a life of Winston Churchill's American mother, Jennie Jerome.
www.annesebba.com

Harriet Smart has published five novels and co-developed the acclaimed fiction writing software toolkit *Writer's Café*. Visit www.writerscafe.co.uk for more information and the chance to download and test out the software. A self-confessed writing addict, she always has more ideas for stories than she knows what to do with, but is currently working on a trilogy set in the 1940s and 50s.

Jackie Steinitz is an economist/market researcher who has written armfuls of reports/trade press articles on subjects ranging from the average weight of passengers at Heathrow airport to the importance of mothers-in-law in diamond-buying in Korea. Latterly she has started writing websites – her first was for her local book group (www.kingstonbookgroup.co.uk).

Aline Templeton's crime novels have appeared in Germany, Netherlands, Denmark, Norway and the United States and in audio form. Her seventh, *Cold in the Earth*, an Ottakar's Crime Novel of the Month, began a series set in Galloway featuring DI Marjory Fleming; it continues with *The Darkness and the Deep*. www.hodderheadline.co.uk

Judge Martin Tucker has spent a lifetime using words at the Bar and on the Bench. In retirement he decided to use the same raw materials to write a book based on a batch of letters discovered after his mother's death, which 'cried out to be published'. He claims to have enjoyed the writing and the self-publishing (but not the search for a publisher in between) and so almost does not mind if it does not sell. *The Chingri Kahl Chronicles* is due in 2006.

John Whitley started life in 1953 and is still going! "I've stopped trying to plan my life," he says. "It's too unpredictable. I fell out of teaching into the commercial training world in 1985 and had more breaks than I deserved. Since then I've been a trainer, consultant, marketer, salesman, managing director and tea boy. So why not author too?" John is married with two grown children and now runs the lead training organisation for the book publishing community.

Jacqueline Wilson's books are both highly acclaimed and hugely popular. She has won the Children's Book of the Year, The *Guardian* Children's Fiction Prize, the Smarties Prize and the Children's Book Award. She is the current Children's Laureate. She is the most famous resident of Kingston upon Thames and is patron of the Kingston Readers' Festival. www.randomhouse.co.uk

Appendix of useful addresses

AN, The Artists' Information Company Exposing the diversity and complexity of artists' practice, AN provides an inspiring critical space to research, analyse and debate contexts for practice now and in the future. 7–15 Pink Lane, Newcastle upon Tyne NE1 5DW, 0191 241 8000
www.a-n.co.uk

The Bookseller Magazine, published by VNU Business Publications, 189 Shaftesbury Avenue, London WC2H 8TJ, 020 7420 6006

The Crime Writers' Association Formed in 1953 as a body committed to the support of professional writers, organises social events so that writers can meet kindred spirits and have some fun together, while at the same time exchanging their thoughts and ideas. They also help writing groups, festivals and literary events with specialist teams of writers who can talk about every aspect of the life of a modern novelist. For information on membership please contact Rebecca Tope, Membership Secretary, CWA
membership@thecwa.co.uk

The Independent Publishers' Guild (IPG) is the membership organisation for independent publishing companies. The primary purposes of the IPG are to promote knowledge about publishing and to provide members with a forum for the exchange of ideas and information. Interesting meetings, an annual conference and lots of good advice available.
www.ipg.uk.com

The Literary Consultancy (TLC) Founded in 1996 and firmly established within the publishing industry, The Literary Consultancy provides expert, market-informed editorial advice to writers at any level writing in English. 2nd Floor, Diorama Arts, 34 Osnaburgh Street, London NW1 3ND, 020 7813 4330 info@literaryconsultancy.co.uk, www.literacyconsultancy.co.uk

Mslexia Magazine for women who write. PO Box 656, Newcastle upon Tyne NE99 1PZ, 0191 261 6656, 0191 261 6636 (fax) postbag@mslexia.demon.co.uk, www.mslexia.co.uk

The National Association of Writers in Education (NAWE) is the one organisation supporting the development of creative writing of all genres and in all educational and community settings throughout the UK. Through publications, events and online resources, members can benefit from the work of their extensive membership network. NAWE, PO Box 1, Sheriff Hutton, York YO60 7YU, 01653 618429 www.nawe.co.uk

National Literacy Trust Founded in 1993, The National Literacy Trust is an independent charity dedicated to building a literate nation. Their mission is to raise literacy standards for all ages, throughout the UK. For more information please contact National Literacy Trust, Swire House, 59 Buckingham Gate, London SW1E 6AJ, 020 7828 www.literacytrust.org.uk

PEN (association for Poets, Playwrights, Editors, Essayists and Novelists) English PEN exists to promote literature and its understanding; to uphold writers' freedoms around the world; to campaign against the persecution and imprisonment of writers for stating their views; to promote the friendly cooperation of writers and the free exchange of their ideas. They run regular campaigns, raising the issues and concerns of members, defending their right to free expression and promoting the free exchange of ideas. The

English Centre of International PEN, 6–8 Amwell Street, London
EC1R 1UQ, 020 7713 0023
enquiries@englishpen.org, www.englishpen.org

Publishing News is published by Publishing News Ltd, 7 John
Street, London WC1N 2ES, 0870 870 2345
mailbox@publishingnews.co.uk

The Romantic Novelists' Association was set up in 1960 to
promote excellent writing and point out to a sceptical world that
romantic fiction is a Good Thing. We are doing well on the first
front with our unique New Writers Scheme and the Joan
Hessayon Award. In this chilly postmodern world we still have
some way to go on the latter, though the FosterGrant Romantic
Reading Glasses Novel of the Year and the Romance Prize
attracted more attention in 2005 than ever before. Conference,
publications, support and members loop. For details of membership, please write to: Hon. Membership Secretary, 38 Stanhope
Road, Reading RG2 7HN
www.rna-uk.org

The Society of Authors has been serving the interests of
professional writers for more than a century. Today it has more
than 7,500 members writing in all areas of the profession –
whatever the specialisation, from novelists to doctors, textbook
writers to ghost writers, broadcasters to academics, illustrators to
translators, writers are eligible as soon as they have been offered a
contract. Invaluable legal advice, ongoing support and an
excellent magazine: *The Author*. For more details contact: The
Society of Authors, 84 Drayton Gardens, London SW10 9SB, 020
7373 6642, 020 7373 5768 (fax)
www.societyofauthors.net

The Society of Women Writers and Journalists is the UK's oldest
Society for women writers. Founded in 1894, aims include the
upholding of professional standards, and social contact with

fellow writers and others in the field, including editors, publishers, broadcasters, and agents. Regular events include workshops catering for our members' specialised interests, visits to places of literary interest, our annual Country Members Day, Autumn lunch, and Christmas get-together, all of which include big-name guest speakers, a biennnial residential Weekend Conference featuring talks, discussions, and seminars on a wide variety of topics, plus biennial overseas trips. For details of membership write to the Membership Secretary, 27 Braycourt Avenue, Walton-on-Thames, Surrey KT12 2AZ
www.swwj.co.uk

Writers' Forum: 12 issues a year on all aspects of writing. PO Box 3229, Bournemouth BH1 1ZS
www.writers-forum.com

Writers' News and **Writing Magazine**, 1st Floor, Victoria House, 143–145 The Headrow, Leeds LS1 5RL, 0113 200 2929, 0113 200 2928 (fax)
www.writersnews.co.uk

Index